The Widower's Toolbox

✦ The Widower's ✦ Toolbox

Repairing Your Life After Losing Your Spouse

By Gerald J. Schaefer
with Tom Bekkers MSW, APSW

New Horizon Press
Far Hills. New Jersey

Schaefer, Gerald J., with Bekkers, Tom, MSW, APSW
The Widower's Toolbox: Repairing Your Life After Losing Your Spouse
Cover design: Robert Aulicino
Interior design: Susan M. Sanderson

Library of Congress Control Number: 2009927401

ISBN 13: 978-0-88282-345-4
New Horizon Press
Manufactured in the U.S.A.

2014   2013   2012   2011   2010   /   5   4   3   2   1

"Unable are the loved to die. For love is immortality."
Emily Dickinson

To my wife Terri, the teacher, who taught me many things, but above all—love. I am eternally indebted to God for sending her to me.

❖ Table of Contents ❖

Part III – Giving Back to Others

Part IV – Loving Again

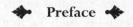

Preface

I never saw it coming. My life was good—really good. I had married my soul mate and we were well on our way toward living a true partnership and raising two wonderful sons. I had just walked five years with my wife through a minefield, doing everything I possibly could to help her defeat breast cancer, only to have the last step blow up in our faces. Terri, the woman with whom I was eagerly looking forward to growing old, died at the age of forty-five.

After Terri's funeral, the task of moving forward in life seemed impossible. A wide range of emotions and thoughts flooded my mind in a seemingly endless sea of confusion. Would I ever be able to endure this grief? How would I manage the daily needs of my family? How would my financial situation change? How could I, as a single parent, continue to provide my sons with the balanced parenting that they had previously received? I felt as if my life was completely dismantled, every component scattered about needing my attention, yet I had no idea where to start to put it all back together. It was clear to me that if I was to achieve peace and happiness again for me and my sons, these issues would have to be resolved. There were repairs I needed to complete to have a functioning life again.

Since Terri's diagnosis was terminal and her death imminent, I was as prepared as a person could possibly be, but it didn't make the pain any less, nor did it make the grieving process any easier for me. I had all the benefits and support systems a person could hope for when grieving the loss of a close loved one. My new employer gave me plenty of time off from work, in spite of the company's dire need of a person in my role. They offered, and I took advantage of, counseling through their employee assistance program. I was also counseled by members of Terri's hospice care program. And I had family and good friends nearby to share in the grieving process and support me.

I had no idea how to grieve her loss, so I tried using the conventional resources afforded to me. I sat through the counseling sessions, read all the literature and even searched the Internet to learn as much as I could to help stop the pain and get my broken life fixed as best it could be. The vast majority of this knowledge came from professionally trained sources, and the information focused on *explaining* the grieving process to me. All the sources described the five stages of grief: denial, anger, bargaining, depression and acceptance. While I believe these stages describe grief accurately, I had no interest in any theories about it. For example, to be told that it is normal to feel angry didn't make the anger go away any faster nor did it make me feel better. It certainly did not help me make critical decisions about my future when I needed to do so.

Discussions with counselors, family and friends only gave me acknowledgment that my life was fractured and their assurance that I would eventually glue it back together. Those who had not experienced the death of a spouse could not provide me with what I felt I needed to hear at that time—a way to sort through and to reassemble the pieces scattered in front of me into fixes that held together. I still felt that my healing process was incomplete. I eventually came to the realization that I had to grieve in a way that would work specifically for me. I discovered that I needed to find a different way to navigate myself out of this mess and gain the wisdom from doing it. I knew nothing would change unless I decided to do something constructive, so I began to reflect more on the best memories I had with Terri. I needed to clarify for myself what she really meant to me and our sons and examine the range of emotions that were keeping me from getting my life back together again.

So as I did this, I formulated by own plan for recovery. The activities found in this book are the ones which brought me relief from my own pain. And as I completed each of these tasks, a little bit more of my wound began to heal. I learned how to glue my life back together, one issue at a time, while seeing a picture of my new life take form. By doing these activities, I was able to take the needed steps toward healing, even if they were more cautious than normal. Completing the activities unfroze me and enabled me to move on with my life.

I rebuilt my life one concern at a time, from the first project of resetting my finances to the last—sending my sympathies to others with handmade cards Terri had crafted. Each was a step forward. Little did I realize at the time, I was fulfilling my "male tendencies" of immersing myself with the work of resolving the issues stemming from losing Terri. These "repair projects" tackled my instinct to become withdrawn by causing me to face the key issues of grief one "job" at a time. As I shared these activities and my experiences with other men who had also lost their wives, I received encouragement to do something with greater impact. I feel I want to share my newfound knowledge with others overwhelmed in their shattered worlds. This book is the result of my desire to help fellow widowers struggling with sorrow.

I truly hope you will find this book to be a guide that will help you gather the fragments of your grief and reassemble them into a meaningful, whole life again.

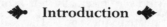 **Introduction**

The grieving process following the loss of one's spouse is, in my opinion, the most personal and difficult experience one may ever face. While the grieving process is very individualized regardless of gender, there are distinctive differences in the manner in which males and females grieve. Men in particular work hard to keep grief to themselves, to maintain emotional control and to refrain from asking for help. Because our culture has created this evolutionary position for men, a "repair manual" that addresses their needs in a manner that integrates with these behaviors can be an effective tool. Simply put, men are wired to continue to fulfill the role society has for them as strong problem solvers who can fix anything including their grief—without asking for help. This book allows men to save face and live within that expectation, because it is written specifically for them in a format of a take-action approach, with the security of a repair reference at their sides.

***

"Hospice told me about a group of recent widowers that met at a local restaurant. I thought I would try it, because in the early days it was really tough being home alone and trying to get a meaningful life back. The group's leader was about my age, but most of the guys were much older than me and I didn't think I had anything in common with them other than being a widower. I actually felt worse after going there, because I just couldn't relate to these guys. They called me and invited me back, but I felt so out of place I told them I couldn't go back. To talk about my grief in front of a large group in a public restaurant environment wasn't my preference. I think talking about it with guys more my age is a much more comfortable thing to do. I also think men and women grieve differently and people need to recognize that—both from the outside looking in and those in grief." –Joe

***

Why could this book help you? It is about occupying your time and mind with activities to honor the memory of your wife while providing a much needed pleasant diversion to lead you from the bombardment of sorrowful thoughts that permeate your mind after your loss. This book helps you move forward with your life by guiding you through the tough issues that you now or may eventually face. You will be performing planned acts of kindness as a method of reflecting on your wife and will come to realize that you are helping yourself and others in the process. Serving others can be a great healer. This theme—being actively involved in making something good happen out of a sorrowful event—will resonate throughout this book. By following the suggestions in the chapters, you will discover new courses of action that will free you from your current fear of surviving your wife's death and motivate you to do things you never dreamt possible. In the end, these activities will make you feel more connected to the memory of your wife in positive and uplifting ways.

The book is comprised of forty-one activities, divided into four parts, which will help you:
- Take care of immediate and basic needs
- Perform personal healing reflections
- Develop your relationships and influence on others

Part I, "Picking Up the Pieces," focuses on activities to get the logistical issues of the household reorganized for as smooth a transition as possible. It provides direction for issues of high importance such as financial and legal changes required to match your new status as a widower. This section also guides you in developing new systems for managing the more mundane but highly critical aspects of a home, such as laundry, grocery shopping and the maintenance efforts of a house. Still other activities focus on tools that you can use to help build your confidence and survive these tumultuous times.

In part II, "Healing From Within," the activities will help transform your grief into reflections of the joy and happiness of the life you shared with your wife. The tasks direct your efforts towards preserving her memory for yourself, family and friends. These activities can also close wounds of regret, expand on the love you shared and even help you decide how to disperse your wife's personal effects to others.

In part III, "Giving Back to Others," we will explore the means to transform the darkness of your grief into a positive light by helping other people rise above their challenges. Others will benefit from the lessons you have learned—from your experiences on how to fight a disease, ways in which to support a charitable organization and even through gifting of personal belongings to those in need.

Finally, in part IV, "Loving Again," you will find a few points to ponder in order to help guide your thinking on the possibility of developing a future relationship.

However, please be aware that you do not have to do the activities in the presented order. Feel free to jump around and pick activities that you feel would be the most helpful and meaningful to do. Use the information as it pertains to your needs and stage of grief.

Within this book there are distinctive dialog boxes that bring in the expert psychological perspective in order to build a technical understanding as to why the specific issue at hand is important for healing. These sections are noted by a subtitle to make them clearly stand out, and they give background as to how men typically internalize and react to specific conditions. This information will often verify for the reader that his problem is very real and seen by many grieving men. In other words, it will remind you that you are not alone.

After finishing each task, complete the reflection questions to capture your experience for possible future review. This can be thought of as a journal of sorts. The prompts transform the advice found in the chapters into a personalized journey by bringing you back to the root cause for your feelings. Feel free to date the entries so that you can track how your personal feelings evolve over this period of reflection. The questions are topic specific in each chapter but are targeted to probe these three simple areas:

1. What were the specifics of the task that I completed? This is meant to capture the details of your experience with this task.

2. How did the task make me feel when I completed it and what did I get from doing it? This will help clarify your feelings that you had during the experience.

3. How did completing this task make me think and feel about my wife? This section allows you to reflect on the connections between this activity and the memory of your wife. The memory of her and how that relates to the task completed is what the final essence of the task is all about. Capture that essence in this section.

Remember that there are many ways in which you can repair your broken existence and move towards a new and fulfilling life. This book is only one tool that you can use to assist your next steps. Completing the suggestions and activities in this book will become a personal tribute to the memory of your wife.

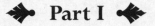

Part I

Picking Up the Pieces

"We shall find peace. We shall hear the angels,
we shall see the sky sparkling with diamonds."
Anton Chekov

◆ Chapter 1 ◆

Contact Other Professionals

When a loved one is dying, one of her strongest wishes is that the surviving spouse will be successful in life and that her death does not cause the survivor undue financial, spiritual, legal and emotional pain. If you and your mate shared these desires prior to her death and planned follow-up courses of action, this foresight will greatly help you stabilize your new lifestyle. You may still want to review the activities cited in this chapter, as they may provide additional insight. If, however, you did not have such discussions with her before your wife's death, and you are left agonizing about what courses of action to take to stabilize your situation, this section can provide you with a good primer that includes insights, tips and guides to start building a new, more secure life.

Emotional anguish will have a strong impact on you and can last a long time. Certainly, the basic steps of planning a funeral and the restructuring of legal and financial affairs are to be expected in the event of anyone's death, but your wife never wished for you to be saddled with ongoing issues or major roadblocks to be resolved beyond those basics. It was her desire for you to move on as quickly and as painlessly as possible in your life. The last thing she would want you to be doing is scrambling through insurance papers, legal paperwork, income taxes, medical bills and other bills while you try to cope with new and old responsibilities.

***

Smarter Than the Average Bear

Widowed men are often confronted with the realization that they cannot fulfill the macho, do-it-all, superhero role that they thought they were playing prior to the loss of their wives. Men have a great degree of difficulty realizing and accepting the assistance of outside professional help. Men simply do not ask for help; after all, history has placed them in the role of being the providers for many generations and this position, while changing, is not going away anytime soon. Thus, many men feel senses of failure if they ask for help, even in areas where they have no expertise! In order for men to move on more easily with their new lives, they need to recognize their belief of pure self-sufficiency is flawed and accepting professional help is a smart use of resources to get certain jobs done well.

***

Ideally, the administrative issues would have been discussed before your wife passed away, but not everyone has this benefit, even when your spouse has had a long-term illness. Important information that requires sorting out includes all investment accounting firms and account numbers, banking (savings and checking) accounts, insurances (both privately purchased and from one's employer), the monthly bills and the household budget.

No matter your level of preparation, the mere act of performing an activity that your deceased wife had done for the family will bring painful remembrances each time it is done until you feel comfortable and adequately skilled in completing those tasks. To gain the skills and the confidence to do those tasks well, you may want to consider seeking assistance in order to make this transition as quickly and as successfully as possible.

Organize your financial paperwork

Financial issues need to be handled first, since the livelihood of the survivors will hinge on adjusting to the new level of cash flow. Locate all of your financial information—both revenue and expenditure related. Start first with collecting all information relating to any source of income: your paycheck, interest bearing (checking, savings, CDs, money market) accounts, investment (stocks and bonds) statements, retirement (IRA, 401k) funds and any other income such as paid rents. Next, collect all information for all debts you may have. These include loans (most regularly for home mortgages and cars), credit card debt and regular utility bills. In order for this process to have a speedy and effective outcome, take time to preview all available information in your possession prior to meeting with the resources discussed below.

Once you have gained an overview of your paperwork, organize it into a readily accessible and easily understood system. If needed, you might want to start a filing cabinet system for all your important papers. Create separate file folders for investment firms, banks, insurance companies, etc. and file each by account name, account number and date. As mail arrives, review and then file it to make it easy to find in the future for tax and other purposes. Simply organizing and filing this information in an easy-to-manage system will remove significant amounts of stress in the future. I have found that filing my documents as they arrive not only improves my ease in managing this important information, but also helps greatly in preparing my taxes.

Set up key appointments and keep them

Now that you have familiarized yourself with and organized your accounts, it's time to get some help in making sense of it all. Set up appointments with key agents who can help you establish good financial practices to prevent problems from developing.

In setting up all of your meetings, ask what kind of documentation you will need to bring. Ideally, they will already have the needed records at their disposal. Find out who will need death certificates. Place information you intend to bring to your meetings in a one-stop location such as a three-ring binder. In the binder, include a pad of paper to take notes for recording your follow-up activities and any questions you generated in preparing for the meeting. The questions list can be drawn up while you are developing your organized filing system. Just jot down your questions as they pop into your head. Don't lose your willingness to ask questions on any topic, no matter how simple the question may be. You need to learn as much as you can, so ask away and have your questions targeted to achieving this goal.

***

"I haven't set up any appointments with an attorney to set up my will yet. It's definitely something that is very important to do and yet I haven't taken care of it. I am not happy about it. Sometimes my procrastination isn't too helpful." —Scott

***

Bring along a support person

Sometimes the subjects you discuss with professional agents consist of consequential details that can easily lead to a lack of understanding and subsequent confusion as to what decisions you should make for your future. The need to make important decisions quickly can become overwhelming and lead to gridlock, which is exactly the last outcome that you would want. If any subject is difficult for you to understand, or you are not in a mindset to insure that your needs are being cared for adequately, solicit the help of a family member or friend to assist you. They might even take on some of those tasks that are extremely stressful and require someone with a clearer mindset and tenacious willpower.

If your wife was employed, you might want to discuss your situation with a former co-worker of hers who may have additional insight in areas where an employee's viewpoint is needed. This may be a union officer or another individual who faced a similar situation as your own. The person may give you a unique perspective, because he or she already understands the employer's system and has had direct experience in working within it. Prepare your questions ahead of time and have your supporting friend along. Remember to keep good notes and keep asking questions to clear up areas where you have a lack of understanding.

A word of caution

When meeting with each agent, try to keep your questions focused on the person's area of expertise. Don't solicit guidance in areas outside the individual's profession, as the answers may differ from those of a trained professional in that subject. You might ask for the person's *opinions* about topics *relating to* the position he or she holds and the experience the person has had, as this may provide some insight to an unforeseen issue. Again, take notes on opinions and suggestions, but confirm those thoughts with the professional who is best qualified in the subject before taking action.

Meet with your attorney

If you do not have one, now would be a good time to establish a relationship with an attorney to set up the future as ideally as possible for your surviving family. There are many legal issues that need to be resolved after the death of your wife. The intent is to build understanding with the lawyer on his or her role in meeting your immediate and future needs. An attorney will tell you all the steps that need to be taken to insure no future issues arise and ensure that your legal status with government agencies is accurately reflected in your records. They are also important because they record and properly execute wills and manage other legal papers such as real estate ownership. The key point is to let their services show you the required steps so that your immediate legal needs are met properly.

Often the execution of the will involves dividing up the deceased's most personal and cherished belongings. Because this can be highly emotional and because such items can precipitate challenges for the inheritors, it is important to convey as accurately as possible the desires of your late wife. Her exact wishes may or may not be clearly enumerated in a will. If her instructions are found in a will, a handwritten letter or even just a written line explaining her wishes about the bequeathed item, it is important to follow through. Your attorney can also assist you in disbursement of personal effects if this activity feels overwhelming for you to complete alone (see chapter 14, "Cherish Personal Effects", for more information). My wife, Terri, wrote a short handwritten note for each of her personal gifts to family members. It made her desires clearly known and therefore unchallenged, while adding a personal touch to the gifts.

Meet with your bank officer

An executive at your bank will help you change your accounts to reflect proper ownership. The banker can also assist you with many aspects of account management depending on the level of services you request. They can help clarify your past cash flow expenditures, loan histories and provide you with a list of accounts you have with them. For example, you may find an account listed only in your wife's name of which you were unaware. Wives sometimes set up emergency accounts for unexpected expenses or even for fun surprises like a trip fund. Some may maintain a personal account in which they keep their company bonuses.

Meet with an accountant

An accountant can be helpful if your wife owned her own business. If so, meet with one as soon as possible. You may need to designate a temporary manager of the business to keep it running smoothly, particularly where employee's incomes and livelihoods are at stake. This temporary manager could be a co-owner or principal officer of the company. An accountant can also guarantee that the books are properly maintained. Your accountant and other financial advisors, if you have any, can assist you if you must make directives regarding company business. Even if you are not involved in a business owner situation, your tax accountant will assist you in several other ways. First, they can help clean up all documentation changes to reflect the proper ownership of your investments to the desired beneficiaries. Second, your tax accountant will ensure that your tax withholdings are adjusted to best match your new cash-flow and tax bracket. Also, he or she will ensure that your new status as a widower is reflected at all appropriate agencies.

***

"I met with my attorney, accountant and CFP to help me restructure my life. Even the funeral home helped coordinate the life insurance payment to me. I found all of them to be extremely valuable as I can't be knowledgeable about all the laws and everything else when someone dies. My advice to anyone facing this life-changing event is to get your paperwork in order. I don't care how you do it. But if you think you can do your own taxes, you're crazy. You might miss something but in this way you will have someone at your side to answer questions if anything comes up." –Jerry B.

**

Meet with a Certified Financial Planner (CFP)

A certified financial planner may be needed to ascertain changes in investment strategy as well as to assist you in changing your investment accounts to reflect proper ownership. Often, investments are changed due to the death of a wife, because the tolerance to investment risk becomes more conservative than when two incomes were at work. If you have mutual funds, you may now wish to shift more funds into longer-term investments at guaranteed returns to avoid having to monitor fund performances. You will also need to discuss with your planner such transfers of ownership to the designated beneficiaries as rollovers of IRAs and other pension programs. The planner can be the same person as your tax accountant but he doesn't have to be. If they are two distinct people, check with both to make sure mistakes are not made that cost you significant tax implications down the road.

If you are not already working regularly with a certified financial planner, you may now want to hire one. If so, get references from other people. As in any important choice such as selecting a doctor, dentist or lawyer, you want to hire a person with a proven record.

**

"I definitely have become more financially savvy since Marnie died. Going through the medical bills and learning about how insurance really works was hard work, but I needed to do it. It's not all good news and you have got to be very careful; for example, I learned a great deal about how 401k plans have nuances to their withdrawal penalties. On the brighter side, I did set up a trust so I can have some peace of mind that things will be taken care of the way I intend them to be for when I die." –Ross

***

Meet with your wife's Human Resources Department

Your wife's employer will typically have a lot of information about benefits for you to understand and act upon. There may be life insurance benefits, pension plans, survivor's income insurance, long-term care insurance or continuing medical, dental and vision insurance for which you and your family may be eligible. The company may also offer employee assistance programs where you and family members can seek counseling for managing your grief. If you have an employee benefits handbook in your home, read it ahead of time to gain an understanding of what might be available to you. This pre-work will help you identify questions you may need to ask, and to ensure all your questions get answered, complete your list of questions before going to the meeting.

The benefits given to employees vary widely and may have many nuances in the fine print. Thus, you will want to ask questions, especially if you do not fully understand what is described to you the first time. For example, the employer may have a life insurance benefit that may be increased by two or three times her annual salary if death occurred while on the job. There may even be additional insurance if the death happened while the employee was traveling for the company. The deceased's employer will share with you who your wife listed as the beneficiaries for the plans in which she was enrolled. This may surprise you, especially if there was a previous marriage and your wife failed to change the records.

A major point for discussion will be the proper handling of your deceased wife's pension plan, if the employer provided this benefit. Proper handling of pensions, which may be extensive, is vital to your long-term financial needs. You may even be liable for payments back to a pension plan if it was used to bridge paycheck gaps, for instance, while awaiting long-term disability benefits.

Finally, ask the company's human resources person who and what agencies have already been notified about your wife's death. This could save you a lot of redundant phone calls and eliminate confusion.

It is very important that you understand your wife's employer's benefits. In my own experience, I discovered that during Terri's long-term disability, a mistake was made in selecting how her pension was to be paid out to her beneficiaries. Only after numerous meetings that eventually involved the teachers union's legal representation was the mistake corrected. This effort resulted in a substantial monetary difference to the benefit of her beneficiaries. While this was initially a difficult problem to resolve, it was my unrelenting drive to keep asking tough questions until I was satisfied with a quality answer that allowed me to solve this problem. This drive coupled with copious notes eventually brought the key players to agree to correct the error.

Meet with your own employer's Human Resources Department representative

Set up an appointment with your HR representative and review the same topics and issues as described previously for your wife's HR department. Ensure that you change your status to that of widower and re-evaluate your benefits to more closely match your new life situation. Such changes may include adding your dependents onto your medical benefits as the new primary carrier. You may even be entitled to benefits from your employer that covered your wife. Again, review your employee benefits handbook prior to the meeting. Such preparation will help you under-stand the sometimes complicated process of benefits entitlements.

Meet with your insurance agent

You will need to provide the agent with a death certificate and your life insurance policy to collect on any life insurance that may have been purchased. Often, an insurance company sells other investment products along with life insurance. Use caution with insurance agents wanting to invest your life insurance check with their firms. A common and simple investment practice is to keep your investments in an easy to understand portfolio and not in numerous locations where it will be more difficult and stressful to manage their performances. Consolidating your funds for ease in transactions, but in sufficient diversity for protection, helps to make your investments easy to understand and manage.

A word about Employee Assistance Program (EAP) counseling

Ask about EAP benefits for the survivors as supplied by your employer. Oftentimes your own employer (as well as your wife's employer) will have counseling available for survivors. EAP provides an accessible safety net that supports the immediate needs of families by helping to resolve their problems through counseling. If in-depth professional help is warranted, they will also provide the family with referrals to specialists. Counseling is also going to be available through a hospice program if there was an illness involved. Many other organizations do a very good job providing counseling support and there is no substitute for professional help if needed. Seeking professional support can bridge many issues and resolve them more quickly than other methods of coping, so do not hesitate if you think you can benefit from it.

Meet with the Social Security Administration (SSA)

Contact your local SSA office (the phone number can be found in your local directory). There may or may not be a benefit for you. Your wife's employer may have mentioned this to you, but call the SSA to be certain you are receiving all the benefits to which you and the beneficiaries are entitled.

Meet with the funeral home director

If you are struggling with some issues several weeks after you utilized the services of a funeral home, consider using them as a resource. Services that you paid for include helping you work through the difficult issues in the transition of losing your wife. They will be glad to assist you. Ask about other agencies that you can contact to help you. The funeral home staff can also provide you with additional copies of death certificates. Get additional copies, because they are more costly to get at a later time.

Meet with religious leadership

Spiritual support following the death of your wife is critically important. Such needs may continue long after the funeral services have ended. In several places throughout this book, it is suggested that you tap into your religious relationships to maintain your spiritual health. But in this chapter, the suggestion is that there may be resources in your religious community who have the skills and knowledge to help you cut through any lingering logistical and financial concerns. Call and visit your local church or religious offices for more guidance.

***

When in Doubt—Contract It Out

Jerry B. and Ross, whose quotes appear earlier in this section, each recognized they required the skills and knowledge of professional resources to get specialized tasks handled correctly. Just like using the right tools for the job, they identified that they could not afford mistakes to be made on important issues. By enrolling experts, they resolved tough issues and were able to eliminate some causes of stress. Each professional they enrolled helped them to lay solid foundations on which to build their new lives, and now it's your turn to do the same.

***

Instructions:

1. Take action and get organized with your financial and legal paperwork. Review your account statements, employee handbooks and other important documentation to build your understanding of your state of affairs. Create a list of questions as you do this review.
2. Set up appointments with the key people we've discussed and keep them. Get answers to your questions and address all life status change notifications that need to be filed. Listen to the advice your professional team gives you. Seek advice from others until you feel comfortable in moving forward.
3. Implement your decisions with their help and maintain those key relationships for future needs that may arise.

Journaling follow-up:

1. What professionals have I utilized and what assistance have they provided?
2. How willing have I been to accept assistance from these professionals?
3. How has the use of the various professionals helped me handle the various responsibilities in my life, particularly those that were managed by my wife?

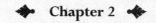

Chapter 2

Enter
Basic Training

When we lose a spouse, we feel an immediate impact through all of the activities she did for us, which we now must do for ourselves: the grocery list, laundry list, social calendar, a seemingly endless parade of bills. We can be quickly overwhelmed by the many basic needs going unmet and the feeling of angst due to major changes in our lives. Family and friends usually help us immediately after our losses, but soon we must pick up the pieces and start to figure out how to do these tasks for ourselves.

We need to figure out a way to get organized with these new responsibilities, so that we can get back on track. I know you are feeling that it is bad enough that we are picking up the pieces, but now on top of that stress, our daily functions are turned upside down. Simple things such as a minor home repair have now become huge challenges to surmount. Finding various coping strategies for such basic needs will reduce this added stress and allow you to narrow the focus on the more painful concerns holding you back. If you can get the basic needs working again, this will help you to heal your sense of loss. A simple method to do this is to develop some basic systems to reduce stress.

***

There is No "I" in TEAM

Some men lose more than their best friends; they lose a nurse, a household manager, a child care expert, a chef and so on. Men who invested themselves primarily in their occupations may experience sudden shock at becoming a single parent. These men may need specific, practical information about how to manage their new roles. A basic cookbook, help in finding childcare and coaching their children to assist with daily housecleaning techniques can help. Health professionals who work with men after the death of their spouses must be aware of the difference in grief reactions between men and women. Women may require more emotional support and encouragement, whereas men may need direction on how to obtain the help they need to manage a household, such as hiring outside help for routine cleaning of the home, cooking and running errands.

The main focus of surviving after a spouse has died is different for men and women. Women express their primary grief response as worrying about how to survive. They also express concerns for their own illness or death, financial stability, loneliness and the loss of the relationship. Men present some of the same grief responses, but their main concerns are survival and performing the daily tasks alone before economic survival. It becomes critical for men to experience some degree of stabilization of tasks and cooperation among family members for eventual renewed harmony within the household.

***

"Robin was the glue." –Scott

***

Before you can feel a stress reduction, you have to get family members to buy into establishing new work systems. This means everyone shares in the stress of the increased workload. Use the new responsibilities as a way to pay tribute to your late wife. Explain to surviving family members that the work needs to be done to maintain the health of the household. Remind others your wife desired everyone's cooperation in making her death as minimally upsetting to the family as possible. As the tasks are being performed, stop and think about this work you are now providing the rest of the family. It is not punishment, but instead a tribute to the deceased's contribution to others.

Start by dividing chores up among all people in the household regardless of age. Break up larger tasks into smaller, more manageable tasks. For example, have a younger child sort whites from colors for the laundry. This simple and easy-to-do activity breaks a huge laundry load into a more manageable one. Assign tasks on ability, frequency of attention required and by equity. Identify roles everyone can play such as a toilet paper/paper towel manager, a recycling and garbage manager, a bill payer, a table-setting-and-clearing manager or whatever else is needed. Everyone can do something for the betterment of the family. When discussions of compensation arise, I have found in my personal experience that the work is the fee for living in the house that we all call home and it wouldn't be fair to expect only one person to bear the entire load. Better still, you might want to consider some sort of a reward system such as a movie night to give incentive to your children and give you some time to relax as well!

Some of the tasks required to keep the household running smoothly may involve skills that you or others simply do not have. This may be cooking, repairing, cleaning or gardening. To solve this, decide on the level of involvement you wish to gain in such an area of expertise, then get training by professionals on a temporary basis until you or your designated family member has sufficiently learned the skill. You may even be able to solicit a family member to help provide the training to save the fee a professional would charge. However, in many instances you may simply not have the availability of tools, experience or the time to take on such tasks that are well beyond your capabilities. In these cases, chapter 6, "Get Help!", discusses how you can trade skills like home repairs for sewing with someone outside the family structure to keep such tasks manageable.

When job responsibilities are identified and broken down into manageable components, whether there is a team of one or more in the family unit, the tasks should be organized into a routine schedule. Rigidity with no room for flexibility is not the idea here; rather, the intent is to develop a pattern you can follow so you know when tasks will be done. This affords you the freedom of worrying about when it will get done. As an example, make Sunday afternoon the day that you do grocery shopping for the coming week. Get into a routine to do one load of wash a day and place it in a laundry basket for sorting. Wherever possible, perform the tasks by spreading them over several days during the week versus letting the work pile up for the weekend. This will help keep you in control if a sudden change in your schedule causes you not to be able to address the task in that day. Finally, the family calendar may be a good tool to help keep other family members on task for a ready reference while the head of the household is unavailable to direct the activities.

Examples of systems to consider include:

- Set up a household calendar: Buy an appointment book at an office supply store or use your personal computer's calendar function. Begin to write everything down on the calendar—all appointments, birthdays, days off from school, etc. If you have one place for all activities to be recorded, that will soon be the master governor to your week's planning. Teach others in the household to write their activities down on it as well. This is particularly true if they expect you to provide them transportation or have some involvement in the activity. If you use a Personal Data Assistant (PDA), it can aid you in planning your work and private life as well. With such a system, you can keep track of all your appointments and even routine functions such as bill paying and grocery shopping.

- Develop a monthly menu: Develop a list of all the recipes that you can cook. Note the major ingredients you need to prepare the meals. If you don't know how to cook, shop for prepared foods such as those found in specialty areas in the supermarket or delicatessen until you decide whether or not you want to learn to cook for yourself. When you do decide, this recipe list will become a master reference guide in developing your grocery list. As you learn to cook or already do, try more recipes and add them to your list.

Sample Recipe List

Meal	Ingredients Needed
Spaghetti	Noodles, ¾ lb ground beef, 3 – 16 oz cans of tomatoes, onion, olive oil, green pepper, mushrooms, Worcestershire sauce, salt, black pepper, oregano
Salad	Lettuce, mixed greens, dressing, croutons, bacon bits, sunflower seeds, shredded cheese, black olives, cherry tomatoes, etc.
Beef Pot Roast	Beef Roast, Flour, Oil, Garlic, Onion Soup mix, Potatoes, Carrots
Sub Sandwiches	Hard rolls, assorted lunch meat, lettuce, sliced cheese, mustard, mayo, tomatoes
Navy Bean Soup	Navy beans, chicken bouillon, onion, potato, carrots, celery, black pepper, salt, bay leaves

This information works best as a ready reference if printed on the back of the shopping form discussed next. By continually editing your recipe list and grocery list as you learn new recipes, you will soon discover that this very important but involved process becomes an easy to do routine. What was once a Herculean task becomes essentially an automated process with few, if any, mistakes.

When I first started routine grocery shopping, I was spending over an hour in the store just to do a week's worth of purchases. Much of that time was wasted developing a weekly menu plan in my head as I wandered the aisles aimlessly. My results were a disaster: too much time, forgotten ingredients, forgotten meal plans and impulse purchases. And it seemed like we had nothing to eat in the house! After systematizing our shopping, I spent less and bought what we truly needed, thus the week's meals were complete and ready for preparation and I was able to scale down my time shopping to less than forty minutes!

***

"Grocery shopping was always a treat particularly if I brought both of my sons. However, I learned I couldn't take them both if I wanted to have an effective shopping trip. I didn't know what to shop for—I initially thought about what I would bring to deer hunting camp. Lots of canned goods in the first year, like Dinty Moore..." —Scott

***

Set up a grocery list form

Discover your favorite grocery store and type up a generic list of food and household items sectioned off as the store is laid out from the entrance to the exit (see example form on next page). Items located at the top of the list are closest to the entrance. Be sure to include all of the ingredients from the menu list you created. This grocery list goes on the front of your menu list as previously discussed. Print out copies of the menu/shopping list and place them in a convenient place such as the glove box of your car or in your wallet. This will allow you to have a form ready to go when you do last minute shopping for the week. To use the form, first decide what meals you plan to prepare for each day of the week and write those meals across the top of your shopping form. Then, reference the back of this form to see what ingredients are required to prepare the meals. Circle those ingredients required from your recipes on the front of the list and shop for those. You will find that your shopping will go quickly, your menus will have variety and you will rarely forget to purchase needed items. After shopping, bring the list home and mount it on the refrigerator. Then your family members will know at a moment's glance what you are having for dinner.

Set up a message center

Purchase a small dry erase board at an office supply store and post it in a conspicuous place in your home. Use it as a place to track family messages and to write down needed grocery items. With a central location, your family can write down reminders about what to take to work or school or even notes regarding completing chores or other

SUN	MON	TUE	WED	THUR	FRI	SAT

Produce

Fruit	Lettuce	Carrots
Celery	Mushrooms	Tomatoes
Onions	Cucumbers	Garlic
Green Pepper	Green Onions	Zucchini
Broccoli	Pea Pods	Avocado
Squash	Pumpkin	Potatoes

Deli / Bakery

Turkey	Ham	Pastrami
Cheese		
Pepperoni	Salads	
Rolls	Lunch Bread	Soup
Bread		
	Italian Bread	
Cookies	Cake	

Pantry

Catsup	Mustard	Pickles	BK Olives	Croutons
Breadsticks	Mayonnaise	Jelly	Peanut Butter	Salad Dressing
Olive Oil	Tuna	Canned Soups	Broth	Pizza Sauce
Pizza Flour	Worcheshire	Soy Sauce	Crackers	Baking/Brownies
Flour	Sugar	Nuts	Salt	Pepper
Garlic Powder	Oregano	Basil	Tomatoes	Tom. Paste
Noodles	White /Red/Black Beans		Rice	Chilies
Chili /Soup/Taco Kits		Fruit Juice	Tea	Fajita Skins

Meat

Ground Beef	Ground Pork	Steaks	Italian Sausage	Chicken Breast
Beef Roast	Beef Stew	Shrimp	Salmon	Walleye

Dairy

Sour Cream	Plain Yogurt	
Pie Crust	Whipped Cream	
Shredded Cheddar		
Mozzarella	Parmesan	Ricotta
Cottage		
Milk	Eggs	Butter
Frozen Peas	Corn	Mixed Veggies
Ice Cream	OJ	Frozen Fruit

Paper/Soda & Snacks

Toilet paper	Paper Toweling	
Lunch Bags	Plastic Lunch Bags	Foil
Saran Wrap	Toothpaste	
Deodorant	Shampoo	
Peanuts	Sunflower Seeds	

Lunch (Special Items)

Dinner (Special Items)

commitments. If possible, find a place to keep blank grocery list forms near this message center so that you can stage an "active form" for the upcoming week. By doing this, you and the kids can write directly on the shopping list those items which need to be purchased on the next trip.

Set up a household chores routine

Laundry, cleaning and yard work are just a few examples of chores that can be made simpler and less stressful with the addition of a routine. For laundry, you may want to purchase additional laundry baskets to hold more clothes until they can be folded and put away. This allows you to keep a continuous flow of laundry moving through the washer and dryer while avoiding the additional task of having to put them away to reuse the basket. Additional baskets can also help as the clothes come out of the dryer, at which time they can be folded and sorted by each wearer and placed in his/her personal clothing basket. When the basket is full, it can be immediately sent to the right bedroom. Cleaning supplies can be organized in a similar fashion by combining all the cleaning products such as glass cleaner, toilet cleaner and paper towels into a single plastic tub or caddy. This approach, which allows you to carry supplies from room to room in one tub, will permit you to save the time that you would have spent looking for products that were left in the wrong location. Yard work is no different. Organize garden hand tools like gloves, hose nozzles and similar items into boxes so that they are easy to store and locate.

***

"I have my children trained pretty well now but the first year was constant training to build their skills and understanding that I needed their help. There were times where we had to have a chat to recalibrate them and sometimes it would cause the boys to cry, but I always explained that we all missed Mom and we have to pull together for her. I have to have more balance now with them. I have to play it on both sides of the fence—firm but nurturing. When there are laundry baskets sitting on the couch they now know they have to handle them. Thank God Robin had a solid foundation laid with our kids that made it easier to get them to come around." –Scott

***

Straighten up your desk

Take a day to organize the central place where you store your bills, checkbook, phone and mailing supplies. First, get rid of all the unwanted or unnecessary items. Throw away the 200 or so pens that won't write any more. Rid yourself of all the free rulers, envelope cutters and all the rest of the junk that just adds to the clutter that prevents you from finding the things you need when you are looking for them. Wipe the drawers clean of broken pencil leads, pencil sharpener dust and the like. You may want to purchase some drawer caddies to keep these office supplies from comingling again. Sort items and group them by function. Place postage stamps, envelopes, packaging tape and all other mailing supplies in the same drawer. Put batteries and paper clips in another. Maybe have gift-wrap available nearby for easy access. Use bins that can help sort bills, school information and even have a place for car keys and your wallet.

For those with children

Set up a basic communication system with your children's teachers to insure their educational needs are being met during their grieving process. You will need to monitor their scholastic progress to insure the impact of their mom's death does not distract them from the importance of getting a good education. E-mail or meet with each teacher personally to establish a method of monitoring their progress during the school year. School systems today have performance and grade reports available online. Teachers will be happy to assist you in this need.

Lastly, stay the course. Things will get better even though they seem overwhelming right now. It will show your children a sense of duty and purpose, role modeling what you want them to see: strength in the face of adversity, self-reliance, all while moving on and respecting their mother.

Instructions:

1. Identify the "new work" that needs to be done.
2. Break it up into smaller and more manageable tasks. Tasks that can be performed quickly are more likely to be completed versus those that require large commitments of time and effort.
3. Assign the tasks—proportionate to skill, equity and availability.
4. Where gaps exist, ask family, friends or professionals to help. Have them come in and train the person responsible for the new responsibility. You may choose to keep the professional staff on board permanently.
5. Plan a perpetual calendar system such as a computerized form to quickly create the tracking system for the next month, thereby eliminating rewriting of repeated tasks. Develop a system to cross off the work item as it is completed.
6. Spread work tasks out over the course of the week versus piling too many up for one day. This way, sudden changes in a day's event will not mess up the entire plan.
7. Use supporting tools, such as a calendar, grocery list, menu and a dry erase board.
8. Share the plan and ask for help. This may require an incentive plan with a reward system (pick a movie, etc.) to gain commitment.
9. Reinforce the plan by explaining that in doing the task, the person is honoring the deceased's memory by acknowledging what she had done for them.
10. These ideas are just a start. Ask friends and family what "systems" they use to keep their lives on track. You will be surprised how many people have a wide variety of ideas that will work well for you. You do not want to be the one stuck doing the job of two people, so get some help.
11. Try developing one of the systems suggested or create one of your own. Pick an area that particularly stresses you. You will undoubtedly see quick results to your efforts.
12. Stay the course!

Journaling follow-up:
1. What specific tasks have I found most helpful in being able to maintain a sense of organization?
2. How have I felt about my ability to manage new systems of performing tasks?
3. How has the adjustment in workload or new responsibilities helped pay tribute to my wife?

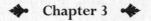

Chapter 3

Establish
New Traditions

The loss of a wife is especially painful during those first holidays. How does a widower move forward without his loved one to reflect on the holiday's purpose, share good conversation, celebrate love and enjoy togetherness? In the beginning, it hardly seems possible. Even though the joy and happiness is abundantly present in others, it's not felt in a widower's heart.

Holidays are highly valued in our busy lives and there are many ways we can choose to celebrate them to meet everyone's desires. Deciding how to celebrate a given holiday, so as to not offend others and to still enjoy this break in our regular routine, can be overwhelming. So we establish routine ways of celebrating them to ease our stress. We justify this same routine year after year by labeling these predictable behaviors "family tradition." We plan dinners at Grandma's house, go to the annual parade and put on display a well-used decoration that just has to be there for the holiday to feel complete. Our holiday memories are centered around such family traditions. Typically, your wife played a major role in these traditions and now with her loss, it becomes blatantly obvious that these celebrations will no longer be the same as they were in the past.

***

"The first Valentine's Day was really, really, tough for me. Long ago as a young man dating Donna, I bought her a nineteen cent Valentine card—it was all I could afford, really. But she later told me it was the first Valentine anyone had ever given her, so it meant a lot to her. From that day on, I gave her a small Valentine as a tradition. Now, on each Valentine's Day, I remember how she always appreciated that small token of love I had for her and it warms my heart to reflect on that." –Larry

***

I Need a Blueprint!

Men generally struggle more with the concept of establishing "New Traditions" in comparison to women as the great majority of traditions center around family gatherings involving a large meal with extensive preparation, in which women have historically been more skilled. Men often become overwhelmed with their inability to solve the problem of preparing an acceptable meal for the family to enjoy and become depressed in their inadequacy. This depression is compounded when a soul mate is no longer there to share a cherished tradition and the "special day" often becomes a painful reminder of the loss rather than a time of joy. The first time you experience holidays or other memorable occasions after the death of your wife, the joy historically felt can now become a nightmare. You may find it helpful for your holiday plan to deliberately include your lost loved one in some memorable fashion. Additionally, creating new traditions will become a meaningful way of channeling some of the feelings of loss and pain into a sense of renewed purpose for you as well as other family members who also may be struggling with loss.

***

Losing Terri hit our family particularly hard in the celebrating of major holidays. Thanksgiving and Christmas were typified by large meals at our home with the extended family in attendance. I was the designated pie maker and responsible for setting up the dinner table while Terri prepared the rest of the meal. In the process, I learned how to make a pumpkin pie from scratch (yes, from a pie pumpkin—not the can). Our home was clearly the epicenter of the family enjoyment for these holidays. Losing Terri changed everything about how we celebrate now. Thanksgiving is now celebrated at my sister-in-law's and I have taken over preparing the Christmas dinner. In a way, this change in our family afforded an opportunity for my sister-in-law to establish herself in a critical role in a new family tradition. This change in routine was never previously approached because it may have been thought too unconscionable to change a family tradition. Whether this rationale has merit or not, I am glad that since my wife is gone, we have established new traditions to keep our family together at these important times of reflection. I now joyfully make pies routinely in the fall and for these holiday meals knowing that it is a symbol of the celebrations we shared together when Terri was physically with us. Though I greatly miss Terri in these special times, I still have a great Thanksgiving dinner, my pumpkin pie and the Green Bay Packers football game to make Thanksgiving a time to enjoy!

***

"We always had Thanksgiving at our house, but the first year without Gloria, my daughter and I made the turkey. It didn't quite turn out like Gloria's used to be but we're learning." –Jerry B.

***

Holiday suggestions

This is a time for you to establish new holiday traditions. If you think about a new way of celebrating the holiday and the memory of your wife, this task becomes easier to create and implement. Here are some simple ideas for you to consider:

- Start by asking your family to have a brainstorming session of new ideas for celebrating the holiday. You might want to share this chapter's suggestions with them. There may be family members who want to start their own family traditions and will now include you and your children in their plans. Don't be afraid to try something new.

- Continue, if you wish, with the established traditions, but also ask other people to help out in the role previously filled by your wife. Split up the tasks by making a potluck meal where members bring one element of the full course meal. Use this opportunity to learn how to cook a turkey as a tribute to your wife.
- Did your wife always carve the turkey on Thanksgiving? This is a great opportunity for the oldest of the children to step in. They can start doing this at age eighteen and continue it until the next child in line turns eighteen. Assign this task to someone to learn and perform it as a new tradition. In the first few attempts, if the turkey carving isn't perfect—relax, it's not that important.
- Start a new tradition by volunteering at a homeless shelter on a holiday to reflect on giving back in your wife's spirit.
- Go shopping for all the fixings of a holiday meal and invite someone over to help prepare it with you in your wife's memory. There are many lonely people who would be glad to team up with your family to share a little happiness during the holidays. You can meet these lonely people through your place of worship or just by asking friends and co-workers to join you.
- Develop a new tradition such as using this holiday period to travel to new places and see how other people celebrate. For example, on the Fourth of July, take a trip to a place where American historical events happened. Make the winter holiday a time for a new family ski trip. Take the key holiday your deceased wife very much enjoyed and use that time to build new and positive memories.
- Employ a professional cook to help you set up the meal the day before the holiday and continue the tradition within your home as your wife managed it. Just get a little help doing it!
- Develop a special prayer for your wife at the time of a holiday. This could be in the form of a candlelight vigil. For example, try this at midnight on New Year's Eve. Use this service to signify starting the New Year in memory of your wife with the conviction of looking towards the New Year with hope.

- Establish the tradition of flying a flag on key dates that were important to her. This can occur on a holiday such as Memorial Day or on a day only meaningful to you and your family. A birthday, anniversary or the day she crossed over can be remembered by flying a flag as a remembrance of the life you shared.

These ideas are just a start as to what you can do to renew your interest in holiday celebrations. If you keep your focus on the importance of the day and turn it inward to what the holiday meant with your wife, you will find that the holidays are survivable.

***

"During the first holidays my kids invited me to stay over at their house to cushion the blow. The holiday meals were always cooked at our house but now they have shifted to my daughters. But lately we have been going to Disney to get away. I've been to Disney five times in the last couple of years—I think I can give the tours now!" –Joe

***

Instructions:

1. Call your family members together to establish some new traditions for those holidays that you and/or your wife previously coordinated. Suggest the ideas in this book, come up with some of your own and be sure to ask the others for suggestions.

2. Be open to changing your plans if new ideas don't seem to be working. It may take a few attempts to settle in on a new process before it becomes a tradition. Give it time to be successful and be willing to adjust your plans as you learn what works and what doesn't.

3. Try different ideas for different holidays. Use the travel idea for non-religious holidays such as Labor Day, for example, to allow you the time to worship in your hometown for religious based holidays. However, keep in mind that the first religious holiday after a wife's death may be the time to get away and to shift your focus toward the pleasing activity of travel.

Journaling follow-up:

1. What new traditions have I tried to establish and who has taken on the roles previously filled by my wife?

2. How well have my family and I adapted to the ideas of these new traditions?

3. How have these new traditions helped keep the memory of my wife alive?

❖ Chapter 4 ❖

Break
Bread

W̵e must breathe, drink water, sleep and eat in order for our physical bodies to function well. This is as basic as survival gets. After the loss of a wife, many men feel extremely depressed, and even these basic survival needs seem overwhelming and of no interest. Eating is the one basic survival activity in which we can invite others to join with us and partake. Sharing meals can provide a much needed boost from others that will not only fulfill a basic need, but will also put us back on the path towards healing.

The sharing of food with one another creates a sense of belonging to the tribe or community. Dining together affords us the opportunity to converse, share and build relationships. Food draws people together, be it at a wedding or a festival where even strangers will gather and enjoy themselves in the experience it creates.

***

Sharing cooking

Through the act of inviting a friend and participating in breaking bread with the other person, men are challenged to move outside of their traditional comfort zones. Most are facing an "out of the ordinary" endeavor which had been a key role of their wives—one of planning and socializing within the context of a meal. Men often comment about their sense of surprise with their willingness to pursue previously foreign cooking and meal event planning skills.

Men who have invested in the coordination of a meal with another are often able to appreciate these opportunities. They recognize this time fosters future relationships that will help carry them through this difficult journey of grief.

***

Soon after you experience the loss of your wife, people often support you by bringing you and your family prepared dinners. This gesture helps to ease the burden of the new responsibilities you must now accept. Receiving a dinner prepared by a friend is itself a helpful gesture that is greatly enhanced if companionship is included as well. Most likely your wife prepared dinners and mealtime schedules. Not only does this responsibility now fall on you, but also your loss is primarily from the lack of conversation and the companionship that comes with sharing meals together. Spending time with a friend and having good conversation over food can be very healing. You can choose whether or not dinner conversation includes discussion of how you are coping with your loss.

***

"Sharing a meal with people actually allows you to step out of the world of grief you're living in and get back into a life that normal people are living. Your thoughts shift away from your grief and your conversation can be just the break that you need—even if for just an hour. You eventually realize however, that the world as you knew it is gone, and now you have to get used to living in the 'new normal' life without a wife and mother. We got so much help from our friends with the many meals given to us that we started to have no place to go with the leftovers!" –Mark

***

One of my most memorable moments in healing the loss of Terri came when I spent an evening teaching a friend how to make a pumpkin pie from scratch. I used to make pies for the family and as I shared this experience with my friend, it brought back a lot of happiness for several reasons. First, I had the rare experience in that difficult time of having fun and good friendship. Secondly, I showed the other person a skill that they appreciated and learned. Finally, my sons saw that the good things we used to do, like making a pie, did not have to end with their mother's death.

The following exercise can be modified to meet several of your own needs by being creative with your friends.

Cook with friends

A great way to have a meal, companionship and reflection on your wife is by inviting a friend over to help you learn to cook your wife's favorite recipe. Use this opportunity to document the recipe for your "Basic Training" initiative from chapter 2 for re-establishing your daily functioning tasks. As you focus on the meal preparation with a friend, you not only share in one another's conversation and companionship, but also you will each learn from the other in the process.

Dine with friends

Another opportunity to move forward occurs when friends call to ask how you are doing or to ask if there is something they can do for you. Invite them to dine with you at your and your wife's favorite restaurant. Use the opportunity of their offer of support to get out and have good conversation with them. Don't let an offer slip by without arranging a time to share in a dining experience to help ease the pain of missing companionship. However, don't wait for others to call you as they may be thinking that you are overwhelmed with offers when, in fact, as time passes following your wife's death you are lonely and alone. Take the initiative and make a dinner date with friends who knew your wife and gave you support when she was ill or right after she died. Use this opportunity to take a moment and thank them for their support. Let them know how a specific act or thought they had shared with you helped you in your time of need. It doesn't need to be an elaborate, well thought out speech; just speak from the heart and say exactly what their support means to you. If you feel up to it, make a toast to your lost love's memory or ask another person at the table to do the honors, as I am certain he or she would be glad to do so.

Take a cooking class

There are many different avenues that can develop your culinary skills and knowledge. Local technical colleges and even restaurants offer classes that have many different formats. You can even take a wine appreciation class at a local wine shop to compliment your newfound skills. This is a great way for you to meet people while learning a basic skill that will help you in the future.

Hold a "My Friend's Best Chili Recipe" party

Invite your friends over to a party where they must bring over a sample of their best chili to be shared among the partygoers. During the party, let all the guests sample the "entries" and judge the samples in various categories: hottest, most Tex-Mex, most unusual ingredients, best white chili, etc. Of course, they must bring the recipe along to be shared with everyone else. Have inexpensive or gag awards for the entrants.

Conduct an e-mail "twenty minute recipe" roundup

Send out an e-mail to your friends asking them to "reply to all" with their favorite "twenty minute recipe." In the e-mail, explain that you are looking for quick and easy recipes to help you prepare a tasty, but quick meal after a long day at work with the key being that the recipe must be able to be prepared in twenty minutes or less (not including cooking time, just the prep time). Anyone who lives a hectic life will be glad to discover new recipes and share in the roundup. Add the new recipes that you like to your menu from chapter 2 ("Enter Basic Training")!

These ideas are just a few ways in which sharing food can be an uplifting means to celebrate your friendships. Be creative and think about some of the needs you might have and turn your needs into a social event. Remember this: The sharing of food with others can mean much more than just eating together. It can be a way to strengthen relationships that are so important in this time of grief.

Instructions:

1. Try one of the ideas in this chapter or create a new idea where you can share the joys of food with a friend.
2. Take the opportunity to thank friends and reflect on what their friendship has meant to you and your wife.
3. Maintain a calendar of those dinner dates or other events and fill it in as people call to offer support. Alternatively, you can call them and arrange for a dinner date long into the future if you wish to do so.

Journaling follow-up:

1. What opportunity have I taken recently to invite others to share a meal?
2. How did the experience of "breaking bread" make me feel as I reflected on my most challenging times of grief?
3. How has the opportunity to share a meal helped me reflect on the meaning of friendship for me and my wife?

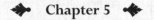

Chapter 5

Seek the
Prayer Connection

Whether you believe in a higher spirit or source of all that is, I believe the concept of prayer or meditation can work for you to overcome grief. Prayer may be defined as a spiritual communion with God or an object of worship, as in supplication, thanksgiving, adoration or confession. If you believe in God, then you already embrace the concept of prayer. If you are a non-believer, I suggest that you utilize the practice of focused reflection, which can be incredibly helpful. When you bring your shortcomings to the forefront of your consciousness, you can improve yourself. You may use prayer, which is discussed in this chapter, as a religious re-centering activity or if you are a non-believer, read chapter 9, which focuses on meditation. The aim of this book is to provide you with the tools for healing from the loss of your wife.

***

Prayer and Meditation

Studies have shown that prayer and meditation can positively reduce the levels of stress hormones in the human body. Such reductions of adrenaline and steroids can reduce blood pressure, heart rate and respiration, thereby influencing the body's immunological defenses against disease. We see a distinct difference in the methods by which men and women carry out prayer and faith in times of grief. Sixty-six percent of women say they pray at least daily, leading men by seventeen percentage points. There are many factors that account for this large gap. Men tend to experience their faith and prayer either by themselves or with a select one or few other trusted people, in a quiet or withdrawn type of environment. Women typically spend more time overseeing children's church activities, are more relational and have a more empirical than rational basis for their faiths. If faith is part of your life, express it in ways that seem appropriate to you. Allow yourself to be around people who understand and support your religious beliefs. If you are angry at God because your spouse died, accept these feelings as a normal part of your grieving process. Find someone to talk with who won't be critical of whatever thoughts and feelings you need to explore. You may hear a person say, "With faith, you don't need to grieve." Don't believe it. Personal faith does not mean you don't talk out and explore your thoughts and feelings. To deny your grief is to invite problems to build up inside you. Express your faith, but express your grief as well.

***

"Because she was in such pain, I actually was thankful when the good Lord called her home and I told Him so." –Jerry B.

***

I believe that prayer is the most powerful gift God has given us, second only to the promise of living an eternity in his kingdom. For me, the concept of prayer is our direct connection to our source. There are facets to prayer: why we do it, when, where, how and what we pray about, but in the end the mechanics do not matter. We do not have to worry about executing our prayers perfectly in order to get results. What matters is that we do it and do it often, be it in good times or in trying times such as these. Whatever the case, prayer makes us dig deep within ourselves to evaluate our issues, where we need help and what help looks like—from our viewpoint of course! During this time of loss, prayer will be centered on issues such as trying to understand the purpose of the loss, the sense of despair and the uncertainty of our futures. We seek guidance through this darkness we are experiencing. Just by asking for help in finding a solution, we release some anguish from our minds and turn a corner to expedient healing.

Prayer, and the self-evaluation that it brings, gives us the ability to re-center ourselves. Prayer provides us that time when we can stop to think about our top concerns and really clarify what is bothering us. We stop and tune into the core issues where we need help. We enter a state of mind where we clarify our needs, ask for help or guidance for resolution and establish a belief towards a positive result. Our mind sheds some or all of the previous stress, and our energy can now be focused on a positive effort. We become tuned into the true purpose of our sacred self and begin to track towards a more fulfilling existence. We regain confidence in our situations and we begin to realize that we will pull through the tough times.

There have been many clinical studies performed on the effectiveness of prayer on improved health outcomes after surgeries as well as mental health issues. In double blind studies, groups receiving prayer did statistically better in their healing process than groups who did not receive prayers. Studies also have been done to test the effectiveness of meditation on healing. The same beneficial effect was found to exist. The power that prayer and meditation have on healing is astounding.

I fully believe through my personal experience that prayer provided a depository in which Terri and I could deposit our worst worries and fears and feel spiritually, emotionally and physically better for doing so. Even though our immediate desires of our daily prayers for beating the cancer were not fulfilled, I know that they were not futile. These prayers brought us many benefits, among them closeness to each other and to God. Our prayers helped to clarify to us that a much larger purpose is governing our lives. I am confident this purpose will all be explained to me one day when I stand before the pearly gates, but I already sense that I am getting my answer each and every day.

If you are a believer or want to begin a new relationship with God, there are many ways to get started enacting the power of prayer and a direct connection with God. Together, these will help you in your healing process. Some examples follow.

Go to a place where you feel a spiritual connection such as a church, a place in nature or another area where you and your wife shared a connection to a higher state of consciousness and being. Get comfortable and clear your mind of the day's stresses. Begin to individually think about the top concerns that come into your thoughts. One at a time identify each problem, why it bothers you and ask for clarity and guidance towards a solution. Repeat this for all the concerns you think are driving your stress. There is no time limit, so go slowly and really analyze each step to make the process more complete. It is best to begin by doing this exercise a few times a week with the intention to eventually do this daily. You will begin to feel that the smaller issues are no longer as bothersome as they were in the past, and you will see the larger issues begin to resolve in your mind.

Visit a location that can provide you with an inspirational setting where you can meditate on your concerns and share them with your higher source. Take a memento from that site (for example, a shell from a beach) and place it in a prominent location where you will see it on a daily basis. Use it as a trigger to reflect a thought of prayer each time you see the item.

You can improve the effectiveness of your prayer by actively learning more about it. Go to a bookstore or library and obtain a book or audio CD on the subject. There is a vast selection on this topic by some very accomplished authors with theological backgrounds. In addition to religious texts such as the Bible and Qu'ran, other books and audio formats can enhance your faith as well.

Consult with your spiritual leaders and practitioners for ideas on how to build your understanding about prayer. Join a prayer circle or prayer group. Engage in a discussion about how they think about prayer, how and when they use it and for what they may be using it. As with anything, the more you practice prayer, the better you will feel about yourself, and the results will be more meaningful and effective. Through routine prayer, you will quickly learn a lifelong skill that can help you every day of your life.

There are additional resources that you can tap into to build your skills and knowledge of prayer for helping resolve grief and daily concerns. For example, use the World Wide Web to your advantage and search out prayer rings. A prayer ring allows you to upload your concern where hundreds to thousands of people will read about your specific issue and your request for help. Members will then pray for your situation to improve. If you believe the connection to prayer and positive results are indeed true, this is a great way to get thousands of people pulling for you. You can also purchase a prayer-a-day calendar and meditate on a different concept each day. Choose to act upon that teaching in some manner for that day.

There is no wrong way to implement prayer. God understands. The important thing to remember is to get started, use it often and continually improve on this incredible gift from your higher source.

Instructions:

1. Make a commitment to developing a habit of prayer or meditation. If this is a new endeavor for you, start with small steps like a simple thought of prayer when you wake up in the morning. Then, graduate to developing a more thorough and consistent approach toward this enlightening practice.

2. Try any or all of the suggestions mentioned in this chapter. You may be surprised at the effectiveness they will have strengthening your sense of spirit and happiness.

3. Create an idea of your own on how to connect to a higher sense of spirit.

Journaling follow-up:

1. What specific ways have I incorporated prayer and/or meditation into my daily reflection or into my higher sense of spirit?

2. How has prayer and meditation helped me grow personally in my overall state of being?

3. How do I feel prayer and meditation have affected my ability to cope with my wife's death?

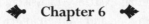

Chapter 6

Get
Help!

Chances are that our spouses did many things for us that we never could have accomplished alone. Their contributions were varied and held significance in life. Because these tasks were completed routinely by our spouses, we often took the fulfillment of these needs for granted. We knew our spouses provided for us, but we didn't really take notice until these benefits ceased to exist. However, now even little problems we encounter such as sewing on a button that fell off a shirt or getting the children transported to a school event become significant issues to work through to get the same results we once enjoyed.

We become overwhelmed and the incomplete projects begin to stack up. The time, money, energy or sufficient skill to do the work of two people is just not in us as one person. Soon, we discover that there are more than just a few instances where we have this shortage of help. We can resolve these issues in several ways: by learning a new skill, finding someone who can do it for us or deciding it just will not get done and accepting that outcome.

***

Get it done

Many men understand the benefit of the mutual exchange of helping one another. Tom states that men's evolutionary wiring causes them to seek opportunities to work on projects together, which creates male bonding time. This desire for mutual exchange in assistance is, in Tom's opinion, a clear difference between men and women in grief. Tom sees it as a result of men's inherent need to complete tasks and build something. A man's feelings of accomplishment by completing a task are heightened by the added value of creating a friendship or deepening an already existing one. This is particularly helpful in the healing process for men who are grieving.

Widowers feel a significant loss in their sense of purpose and self worth, but go on to quickly repair these feelings as they repay others with completed tasks. This mutual offer of assistance reinforces their belief in the altruistic nature of mankind.

***

In chapter 1, we discussed how to get professional help on the tougher issues such as resetting your finances and legal status. Of course, hiring professionals involves fees. In chapter 2, we gave our ideas on how to enroll your family in resetting the basic daily tasks for the household activities, albeit acknowledging that there is a limit to what your entire family can deliver. This chapter is aimed at the very specific purpose of creating new friendships or developing the ones that you already have so that you can work together to achieve mutual success. That is, by being a good neighbor, you can get things done without writing a check.

You may know someone who has the skill to provide professional results to meet your newly discovered needs. Such opportunities can evolve into a larger benefit of creating a new relationship that may allow you to continue to utilize this resource in the future as you need it. For example, if spring-cleaning your windows or another household chore is necessary, a neighbor may be willing to provide his or her services in exchange for something you could provide, such as shoveling snow or cooking a dinner. There are many women who are proficient in domestic skills, such as sewing, who may need someone to help them with small home repairs. Each and every need can be viewed as a means to meet new people and gain new relationships.

I was glad to return the favor of a friend who helped me greatly shortly after Terri's funeral. She, along with two other friends, helped me put together the scrapbook of Terri's more memorable moments—something that I was anxious to do. After several scrapbooking sessions, the scrapbook was completed and I was very satisfied with the results. I felt deeply indebted to them for the guidance they gave throughout the project. Later on, one of the women wanted to purchase a new car. Since her husband was not interested in pursuing all of the car shopping and data gathering required to get the best car for the best price, I was glad to help her in this endeavor. After a few excursions to private sellers and dealerships, she ended up purchasing a car that she originally thought would not suit her taste. But after thinking it over, she did take my advice and got a terrific deal on a very nice car. I was very glad I had been able to return the favor of helping me create Terri's scrapbook and witness my friend's happiness in enjoying her new set of wheels.

The suggestions of friends, family and co-workers can yield some very good leads to reputable businesses that can meet your needs. When establishing the relationship the first time, use good judgment in what to share with the person about why you need their assistance. Do this until you are convinced he or she is a person who provides good value to you (value meaning quality at a fair price). Once you are satisfied that the person is reputable and produces quality services, work in an explanation as to why you need assistance. As you begin to routinely do business with the person, you may find that he or she will be willing to "go the extra mile" to satisfy you because of your situation. You may also discover that he or she is also in need of a service you could provide. Use this as an opportunity to return the favor.

***

"I have learned to be much more appreciative now for the little things people do for me and in turn, I think my willingness to help others out has grown. Showing appreciation with a thank you followed by lending a helping hand goes a long way in building relationships." —Mike

***

Remember that not all needs have to be serviced by payment to a professional; there are many creative ways to develop sharing relationships with others, leveraging your own skills in trade. Think about this the next time someone mentions your special talents and use them as barter for getting your next tough job finished!

Instructions:

1. Develop a "punch list" of items of work to be done that your wife had previously completed for you. Next to each item, write down the names of those you know who may be able to complete that specific task. Ask that person if he or she would be interested in working out an arrangement for completing the task on a regular basis.

2. You may choose to let the work pile up and have the work done at once by one resource for a larger payoff. Often, a better price can be had by grouping several projects together to make it more attractive to the contractor.

3. Check the newspaper classified advertisements for resources you might need and ask the advertisers if they are willing to accept offers of trade. Your trade may be services you can provide or bartering to get rid of items no longer being used.

Journaling follow-up:

1. What are examples of when I have accepted help from others and also offered to help them in return?

2. How did I feel about accepting help, in addition to providing a service or favor in return?

3. How well have I viewed these opportunities to accept help as a means of meeting new people and gaining new relationships?

Chapter 7

Get a Body/
Mind/Spirit Tune-Up

Soon after the death of your wife, the depth of the loss on you and others who knew her is recognizable. Immediate family, friends and co-workers may feel the vacuum left behind so strongly that there may be lingering questions as to whether her death could have been avoided by some preemptive actions.

The loss is particularly painful if the death was the result of an illness that could have been averted or discovered sooner and treated successfully. In such cases, thoughts of anger may arise in the minds of those left behind. This may or may not have been true, but survivors often think that death was preventable regardless of an unfavorable prognosis. In the case of a sudden and untimely death, the frailty of our existence is made much more evident to us than ever before. It serves as a "wake up call" to our mortality. We are constantly informed of the most recently discovered lifestyle health risks and we worry about predispositions of disease in our genetic makeups. Nevertheless, in our grief, we may skip that annual physical, postpone seeking treatment for a lingering ailment or even skip routine maintenance like dentist appointments for teeth cleanings. And though we may be secretly wondering about our own health, choosing not to act upon simple preventative activities makes a

statement to our loved ones that we are selfish, fearful or have an ignorant mindset. How we answer these "wake up calls" may be the most
significant choices that we can make following the death of a wife.

***

Check with the Data

Men and women grieve differently. Men are more likely to exhibit
injurious behaviors such as withdrawal from others, increased drinking,
increased smoking, poor eating habits and physical inactivity. Many
bereaved men actually recognize this increase in such destructive behaviors and still do not adjust their behaviors accordingly. Left unchecked,
widowers exhibit more mental health problems, severe illness and even
suffer greater mortality than widows. Men can learn some basics from
women, because women typically have better skills in food preparation
and rely more on friendships and networking to keep their spirits lifted.

***

After the loss of a wife, action must soon be taken for the simple
purpose of completing the work our spouse entrusted us to do, particularly if young children and other dependents are involved. Children
may become very nervous and worry that with only one parent in their
lives their futures are uncertain should something cause the death of the
remaining parent. They may become preoccupied with their future well-
being, but may be reluctant to discuss their concerns over who will care
for them. Your health and well-being need to be high priorities for the
sake of your family members as well as you. As the survivor, you need to
take steps to insure that you are doing all you can for your dependents. If
there are no dependants, you still need to do this for the sake of other
family members who also see you as an integral part of their lives.

Unlike typical health improvement plans, this health intervention
builds upon the three cornerstones of body, mind and spirit as a way to
"tune up" the whole body. One can have any two of the three in place, but
without the third, one's life is far from being whole. The world is filled
with people in top physical shape but they are distressed by relationships

and self-doubt. Similarly, people can be very spiritual and be centered with their purposes in life, but be physically unable to participate in many functions important to them and their family lives. Hence, regardless of the incomplete mix that may exist, there are many ways to fill in the gaps.

Even before Terri's death and for a while afterwards, my total health picture was scattered like a jigsaw puzzle still in its box. The pieces were there, but I didn't recognize this, much less feel I had the time to work on my own well-being. After all, I had two sons to comfort and care for among other pressing issues requiring my attention. In my grief, I failed to remember how these pieces connected with one another. By doing so, I would have been much more empowered to getting myself back together and therefore been able to help my family more effectively.

My first visit to my family physician after Terri's death allowed me to reset my cornerstones so I could rebuild my health upon them. In meeting with him, he explained how the body-mind-spirit interconnection is crucial to one's overall health. In spite of my own personal experience in the importance of each of these foundations to my life, I needed to be reminded of the need to put it all together and by concentrating on just these elements, the rest of my concerns began to fall into place. Sometimes we have a "blind spot" when it comes to seeing the obvious solution to a problem until someone else calls our attention to it.

The body tune-up

Ratcheting up your responsibility for proactive health management can be made into a special event. Schedule a day to consolidate all your family's medical records if they are in numerous locations. Medical records can be easily fragmented. This can happen with frequent changes in health network providers or physicians. Ensure that you verify that your health records have arrived and are complete. Often, depending on the size of your medical records and the associated time and cost to reproduce the file, offices will only send basic information, leaving key documents behind. They assume that the requestor will ask for the additional information when he or she needs it. Remember that it is your record and you are entitled to all of it. Records to ask about include: immunizations, family histories, imaging files and specially ordered test results.

Once all of your records are organized with your primary care provider, establish appointments for physicals for all members of the family. Make it a designated family health day starting with a well-balanced breakfast for everyone, the physicals and then cap it off with a family walk. Do the same for a family dentistry day and optometry day. These appointments can be made annually and coincide with annual fundraiser walks for a charity of your choice. In doing so, you can combine your interest in addressing your own family's health management while helping someone else's health in the process.

During your appointments, be proactive and ask your health care provider for advice on how you can improve your health. Take notes and ask for any literature he or she may have that would be good reference materials for specific topics of concern. It is one thing to know what the opportunities are, but it's another to do something about them. Acting on this health assessment information is important.

I am not coaching you to become an Olympic athlete to fulfill this objective. You can make changes gradually and feel good about small successes, then, if you wish, move on to more significant changes. For example, start improving your health by simply making healthier choices. Reduce caffeine and sugar in your diet to facilitate better sleeping and general health. This will be especially beneficial in the early stages of grieving, as sleep will be difficult due to the high levels of stress. To stay on track, dedicate this small change in lifestyle to the memory of your wife. To further develop better sleeping patterns, listen to audio CDs of nature sounds while falling asleep. After putting some of these simple changes in place, you might be ready for the significant change of a full commitment to a workout regimen. If you already are doing this—great! If not, go to chapter 21 for some suggestions on how to get started.

***

"Shortly after Donna passed away, the quietness of the house and my need for companionship made my feeling of loneliness unbearable. I decided to take advantage of a special rate at the orthopedic center for seniors just to occupy my time. I now work out three days a week because I do have more time on my hands and it is a great way for me to get out and socialize. Working out has definitely helped me in more ways than just physically. Of course it builds your body up to where you will simply start to feel better, but equally important is that it occupies time away from the doom and gloom of grief. It also builds new friendships in the process. It would be real easy for me to stay at home, sit in the easy chair and sulk about what happened to me, but I have learned that I can go to the gym, work out and still talk to people about losing Donna. At the end of my workout I feel much better about myself and my situation—it's good therapy!" –Larry (married fifty-one years, age seventy-three)

***

The mind tune-up

Of the three foundations to total health, achieving good mental health seems to be the most difficult to define. How do we feel emotionally within ourselves and outwardly in our relationships with others? How does anyone assess his/her own state of mind? What does a completely healthy mind actually feel like, and is there ever a true endpoint to know when we have achieved it? The short answer, I think, is that there never is an endpoint. We are always a work in progress. When we can completely let go of the ego, the daily stress that comes our way and the non-productive inner dialog incessantly repeated to us, only then can we envision an endpoint. Other than a select few on the planet such as Sister Teresa, the Dalai Lama and other such influential people, who themselves have admitted to the challenges of maintaining inner peace, we should think in terms of living towards this vision one day at a time.

These questions will continue to be there throughout our lives, but the first step in developing a healthy mindset after losing your wife is simply to pay it the attention it deserves. Taking time to relax, actually meditate and listen to our inner voices is a simple and quick check to assess our mental well-beings. Chapter 9, "Learn to Meditate", gives ideas on how to learn the skill of meditation and chapter 10, "Use Affirmations", illustrates how to learn the technique of listening to and controlling one's inner dialogue. If you find yourself struggling to get into the "zone" of a peaceful mind, this is a clear indicator that you need to repair this foundation of your total health. If insomnia, knee jerk reactions and missing commitments that let yourself and others down could be used to describe you, then maybe it's time for a mental tune-up.

***

"The connection of the mind to physical health is definitely real. It is amazing how stress can mess you up. I developed a heart arhythmia problem from all the stress I was carrying with me. I was in real trouble because my heart would go into these episodes of fluttering versus having good solid contractions. During one episode, a doctor was simply amazed I was still conscious because my heart was struggling so much. When I saw my heart fluttering on a monitor, I found that I was able to control it by thinking about slowing it down. That, for me, was the proof in the pudding that I needed to exercise and focus on the health of my mind as much as the health of my body." –Scott

***

There are many ways beyond meditation and affirmation that can help you to tune up your mental health. Set up some time utilizing your employer's EAP center or call the hospice that may have worked with your family. Even though it may have been a while since you last spoke to them, find out if there is a support group that may be available for continued discussion if you feel that such steps might be beneficial. You may even find that you may have something to offer another person who may need your advice. Being asked for your opinion can be a very satisfying experience for improving your emotional health.

***

"Losing a wife is like going cold turkey from a drug addiction—it's tough, really tough." –Rick

***

Optimum mental health includes thinking about your children's needs as well. Some health centers have well-trained experts to address children's concerns and you should take advantage of them. The opportunity to speak honestly and openly with your children may be valued even more so than talking with a stranger. However, your approach should vary with the age of the children involved. For example, you may share with your children what will happen to them should you, the last parent, die. Let them know who will take care of them and from where financial support will come. Let them know you have thought this issue through and you will not leave them without someone to care for their needs. Do not feel the need to go into details, but reassure them that other adults are set up to care for, comfort and love them should something happen to you. Of course, be sure to have these concerns legally taken care of before making such promises to a dependent.

Another way to increase your sense of emotional health is to simply take time for yourself. Release yourself from the pressure of not only losing your wife, but also from the daily pressure of trying to readjust to your new existence. Try a hot whirlpool or soaking bath with lighted candles nearby and reduce your stress by tuning out the world for a moment. Use this time to clear your mind and practice emotional relaxation. This is a great time to practice your meditation skills described in chapter 9.

The spiritual tune-up

Last, and by no means least, spiritual health tune-ups are also needed. If you have religious faith you should ask: How healthy is my spiritual relationship with God? You might want to reflect on your frequency of prayer and attendance at your place of worship. Chapter 5, "Seek the Prayer Connection", and chapter 8, "Become Inspired", have several ideas to get you back on track in these areas. If your attendance at your place of worship has fallen, get back into the fold and worship as a routine part of your week.

***

"I can't blame anyone or God for why Kathy died—it just happened. Blaming is not going to do you any good." –Rick

***

If you do not have a regular place of worship, establish a relationship with one or with another organized spiritual group who can serve to uplift your spirit. A way to jump-start this would be to ask a friend where he or she worships and go with that person.

***

"With faith in God and memories of your life together you are going to be able to carry on. It's going to get better. If you are not a religious person and don't have a good place to lean on, check out 'Griefshare' or group counseling as a way to find a good support base. For me it was my walk with the Lord that helped lift me up." –Larry

***

Make a point to set up an appointment with a spiritual advisor. You don't have to have a specific problem to resolve, just use the time to discuss anything that may come to mind. A great idea is to invite a potential or present advisor to lunch in order to build your relationship with him or her. Religious leaders can be excellent resources due to their training and experience. They may even point you toward people within the spiritual community who have suffered similar losses with whom you can share your thoughts.

If you don't share in the beliefs of a higher source, then you might want to ask yourself how healthy are your relationships with the people around you at work, home and with your extended family. What are you doing to improve those relationships and feel more uplifted in spirit on a regular basis? Practice your self-reflection meditations and affirmations. Spiritual tune-ups can be done in a number of ways, such as increased levels of personal reflection, spending personal one-on-one time with trained professionals or simply by reading inspirational literature.

Working toward strengthening a healthier body, mind and spirit ensures that the engine that drives your daily life is well tuned to finish this endurance race of grief. You will react to tough issues with greater confidence of successful outcomes knowing that you have the horsepower and fuel in your tank to help yourself and the others you love.

Instructions:

1. Try the ideas listed in the chapter. You don't need to do them all, but be sure to choose something to do in each of the three areas: body, mind and spirit. You want to be true to strengthening each of these three foundations so that your new existence is built on solid ground from all aspects of total health.

Journaling follow-up:

1. What specific steps have I taken to ensure my physical, mental and spiritual health?
2. How do I feel other family and friends have benefited from my efforts to attend to my physical, mental and spiritual health?
3. How has my overall sense of well-being been affected by a greater awareness of the role of body-mind-spirit?

❖ Chapter 8 ❖

Become
Inspired

As men, when we are faced with sobering questions related to the meaning of the loss of our wives, we may recognize the need to embrace the often uncomfortable concept of connecting with our spiritual side. Men as a group claim less spirituality than women. Men tend to struggle with the idea of being "in spirit" as this challenges our sense of purpose beyond that of the family—that of our worldly spiritual existence.

This ability to venture toward a mindset of inspirational thinking provides men the opportunity to evaluate beliefs and values, both as we live a mortal life and as we face beliefs relating to our wives' connection to a higher being.

In this chapter we see Scott and Rick experiencing this challenge as they strive to live their lives inspired by Robin's and Kathy's spirits, knowing that they are still connected to them.

***

You may believe in a divine being or you may not. Regardless of your belief system, after the loss of a loved one, it is only normal for your spirit, or sense of purpose in life, to feel bereft. By now you have probably already heard of and experienced many stages of grief and have been told that a broken spirit is a normal response. Ongoing questions abound in your mind: *Why did God allow this to happen? Why me?*

How am I to feel any inspiration divine or otherwise, after this happened? Then again, you might feel a higher sense of closeness with a divine source. However, there is no doubt that your broken spirit will take on many different forms, such as anger and depression, as you grieve. In your depression, you may have a feeling of disassociation with God or the people around you. You might think that they simply do not understand what you are feeling. You may feel that the day's tasks are unimportant in comparison to things that really matter like the loss of your major relationship. You can help regain your purpose in life by turning to your chosen religious scripture or other affecting literature for inspiration.

***

"There is definitely a higher being that I know is helping me. I was very, very, very angry when she got her cancer. I was pissed. I'd ask Him, 'What the hell are you doing to me? Don't you know what's going on? There are a lot of people praying down here to have you fix this.' Yet it never changed for the better. Eventually, you get to a point when you accept it—but not quite. Then, there are times when I'm hitting some tough points and I need some kind of miraculous intervention. Suddenly out of nowhere it comes and the situation resolves itself. That's how I know she's up there working with Him to help me out." –Scott

***

The intent of this chapter is to direct you to literature to find inspirational messages that can help you develop a renewed sense of purpose in life regardless of your religious beliefs. If you do not share the same viewpoint as I do in a divine source, I ask you to think about the following as you read this chapter. Where I choose to use references to scripture and God, ask yourself what writings and motivations cause you to seek a higher sense of self. This chapter challenges you to reconnect with those references to rebuild an inspired life. For example: the key theme I want you to understand is: Get close to inspirational thinking, internalize it and your spirit will return.

There are many ways I maintain my sense of connectedness to God to keep me inspired. A simple thing I do is to pray every night when I climb into bed. Some days, I feel so exhausted that I just do not have the energy to run down a list of issues where I need His divine intervention, so I simply ask for forgiveness for that day's events and I also ask to become an instrument of His peace. Even in that short amount of time, I feel my connection is renewed though it is just a brief moment of prayer.

Another way I stay in spirit and one I find great satisfaction in is reading scripture to the members of my church as a lector. I start by reading the lessons for a particular Sunday a day or two ahead of time so I don't embarrass myself with poor pronunciations of Biblical names and exotic places! This practice time really affords me the opportunity to listen to the message God wants me to hear. By studying it closely so I can deliver a dynamic reading, I am rewarded with a message that is more meaningful and memorable for me to live by during the upcoming week. A better solution is to find a way to do this more routinely. Hence, I select a line of scripture that I find particularly inspiring. I read it every day and, when I feel a change in my need to feel inspired, I find a new one and replace it with that passage.

A great way to live inspired is to have a theme to focus on for a day or even just a part of the day, where you can slow down and clear the clutter from your mind. If you turn to a spiritual resource such as the Bible or similar inspirational writings that have withstood the test of time, you can find many themes on which to focus. A great way to do this is to purchase a daily flip calendar with a passage from scripture as a reminder to focus on that theme for the day. Every time you glance at it, take a moment and reread the message. The day's stressors will seem to have little impact on us because we can rise above them with our focused sense of true being.

Not into scripture? Reconnect with the great literary masters and pay particular attention to the poets, for their eloquence can inspire you by striking just the right chord. Your local bookseller can help you make a selection based on the purpose you share with a motivating author. William Shakespeare long ago wrote of the concept of being singularly focused on what counts in our daily lives. I believe this to be a timeless concept of inspiration that we should apply to ourselves today. "To thine own self be true," he wrote in *Hamlet*. Shakespeare's quote does not mean to tell others what you think of them every minute of the day. I believe it means to focus inwardly on becoming the best person you can become. Pay attention to your development as an individual and all other issues will fall into place. The secret is to know that no matter what the overwhelming tasks in front of us may be, we have the strength to survive it because being inspired keeps us centered on the important work.

Another idea to share the benefit of such thoughts is to select greeting cards that have inspirational messages in them. Send the card to someone whom you think may be in need of the message and it will brighten both of your days.

One more key method to become inspired again is to really improve your understanding of inspirational literature by joining a study group. These groups meet to study literature at bookstores and others delve into scripture in the form of study groups at places of worship. Learning about the background of a given passage and other details concerning it will allow you to reconnect with your inspired spirit in a communal environment.

***

"Kathy made me a much better person than what I was before I met her. I feel much more connected to God and my religion because of her. There is a special church in Bangkok, Thailand, that she loved where I feel close to her and to Him. If I die tomorrow I'm fine with that, even though I'm leading a happy life now and do a lot of fun things. I don't worry about anything because I know I'm going to see Kathy someday." –Rick

***

Recapturing your inspiration is not necessarily an easy thing to do. Don't subscribe to the popular argument that only time will heal your loss of inspiration. You have to invest in yourself. Even though it might feel like work at first, the rewards will be great and will be lasting. When you are able to shift your focus from trying to accomplish every last earthly task for the day and re-focus on living toward your true self, you will become enriched. You will feel renewed and the relationships around you will improve, because you are actively focused on your life purpose and consequently, externally to others. Living such an enriched, purposeful life will help you reconnect to the spirit of your wife.

Instructions:

1. Purchase a daily inspirational calendar that contains a message or scripture passage for each day of the year. Read it and take five minutes to decide how you will act on that theme for that day. Make a concerted effort to make it real.

2. Volunteer to be a reader at your place of worship. Reading scripture to others can be a rewarding experience because it places you in a position to learn the passage for later recall, helps to develop public speaking skills and, most of all, will give you the joy of sharing spiritual information directly with others.

3. Next time you look to purchase a greeting card for some event, select one that has a spiritual or inspirational message on it. Find new opportunities to share these powerful messages.

4. Join a study group at your place of worship, local bookstore, library or educational institution. Or, if there is none, start one! There are many study guides available that can help lead this newly formed group. Discuss with others what you have learned from reading inspirational literature. This will also be a great way to socially interact with others who share the same interest.

5. Add an inspirational message to your affirmations card (See chapter 10, "Use Affirmations"). Be selective by choosing a passage to fit your current need or go out on a limb and have one of the many sites on the Internet send you one by e-mail. Sometimes a random passage will help you think of something you might need to reflect upon but would not have thought about on your own.

Journaling follow-up:

1. What steps have I taken to become involved in regular, inspirational reading or community spiritual activities?

2. How have these inspirational activities helped to strengthen my relationship with God?

3. How has my sense of purpose in life been affected as I look to the future without my wife?

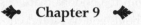

Chapter 9

Learn to Meditate

Meditation is a state of concentrated attention on some object of thought or awareness. People envision meditating in many different ways. Some of us picture ourselves high up on a mountaintop wearing a thin shred of clothing, sitting in a crossed-legged position and reciting a mantra to ourselves. For others, it can mean thinking deeply in solitude in order to resolve an important issue or recharge one's mind. However, some have never meditated at all and might wonder why a person would waste valuable time apparently doing nothing constructive.

The benefits of mediation are chronicled in many different sources for many different applications. Research has shown that meditation improves the health of people confronted with deadly illnesses and is a significant influence in reducing personal stress. It is widely accepted that stress is the single largest cause of disease. The actual word disease is formed from disease, your body not at ease within itself. Many credit meditation with being the source of significant improvement in personal performance in sports as well as the reason that they have achieved financial and personal relationship milestones. Meditation frees your mind to achieve a moment of true peace. When experiencing the sorrow of a wife's death, meditation can be the single most important tool that will wash away negative energy from your mind, while bringing clarity to what was valued in your relationship.

There's a saying from the Buddha that goes, "Know well what leads you forward and what holds you back, and choose the path that leads to wisdom." He is asking us to clearly identify what barriers prevent us from being whole, and then to let go of them. Our negative thoughts, endless worries and constant daily pressures foul our minds from the start of each day and last until we go to bed at night. Taking the time to cleanse these from our minds allows us to stop and hear, even for just a moment, what we really want and need to focus upon. Our minds are filled with self-dialogue that drowns out our important core thoughts. All day long we think about what we should or should not do, what task is next, what time it is and if we are running late. Most disturbing are the things that we do not tell ourselves to do—be patient, help others or empathize with those around us. When we focus on the richness of pure and positive thought, we begin to understand what direction we should take in order to be on the path to true wisdom and enlightenment. Worries will begin to fade and stress will evaporate as we can let go of non-serving thoughts and finally hear the thoughts that have a constructive purpose.

With practice, you can be so self-assured that no matter what issue tries to drag you down, you can be carefree because you know that a positive outcome is forthcoming. With this new perspective and state of mind, you will quickly notice that most everyone with whom you interact will add positive experiences to your day.

With the loss of your wife, it is too easy to dwell on all that is bad and negative in your life. You are bombarded by examples everywhere you turn and reminded that you are no longer whole. You must acknowledge these feelings of loss and sadness, but you cannot do so at the expense of never taking the time to reflect upon the thoughts of fulfillment and happiness your wife gave you as well. In fact, you do dishonor to the memory of your wife and the life that you spent together by only remembering the hurt and not acknowledging the joy and happiness that she gave you. Meditation will allow you to shed the dark sense of loss and resurrect the shining love you shared for each other.

***

Go with Your Gut

Men in grief tend to keep their pain to themselves. We appear to others as not needing to communicate about our grief. This form of non-communication serves as protection against being viewed as vulnerable and non-masculine, which is the expression of grief through tears, feelings and sharing.

Why do men act in this way? Men are inward thinkers, seeing the situation and not the emotional responses. This does not make us less emotional or less responsive to those around us, we just have different methods of processing the emotional response. The closer you are associated with a man in grief, the less likely he will share his grief with you. His "job" of protector does not allow this vulnerability to be exposed.

Because of a man's natural inward perspective, meditation can be a natural fit and powerful tool for healing. Meditation bestows the time to purge the day's stressors from the mind and shift focus on being at peace in the moment. In effect, it is personal grief time that allows the bereaved to listen to his heart on thoughts of most importance to his healing. Tuning in to the emotions and thoughts of their own hearts will make it easier for both men and women to accept grief support from others. They need to hear reassurance from others that their emotions are normal, their responses to these emotions are normal and that they will be able to live and love again.

***

"Rely on your friends, family or pastor to get through this. Talk to them and express your feelings. You have to get your feelings out because sucking it up just doesn't work. You may think you can suck it up, like you're some kind of a tough guy, but in the end it comes out anyway. Getting in tune with your real thoughts and feelings is a healthy thing to do." –Mike

***

I learned the power of meditation when I was faced with a serious medical condition instigated by the stress of my job. My stress level affected my eating and sleeping habits to a point where I could not fully function during everyday activities. This condition developed over several months and I lost a significant amount of weight. After numerous tests and medication trials, I was told I would have to take a powerful prescription drug for the rest of my life. Hopefully, the medication would address the issue, but if the condition worsened, I would be on a path for a surgical solution.

I knew my thoughts had created this condition; after all, it was my internalization of how I perceived my work environment that was causing the stress. Because of this belief, I felt that if I could change my mindset, I could heal myself. To say I was given long odds is an understatement. After making a total commitment to meditating my stress away a minimum of three times each day, I was able to go cold turkey off the medication to the surprise of the medical specialists caring for me. While it took about a year to make a full recovery, I could feel my condition improving almost immediately.

At first, meditating gave me something to do while I was attempting to sleep but couldn't. Then slowly but surely it allowed me to reject the negativism of my job and to disown the shortcomings of my work environment, which I was powerless to change. I fully accepted my role and responsibilities but was now creating a mindset that I couldn't be the captain of the dysfunctional world in which I was working. The more I meditated, the better I felt and was able to more fully function for my company. In the end, I was able to be a key person who pulled the team through a difficult situation to success. While it took about a year to make a full recovery, I strongly believe that learning how to meditate and cleanse my mind from daily negative clutter saved me from a serious medical outcome, and it now gives me a means to more fully enjoy my sacred sense of self.

Getting started in utilizing meditation to silence your grievous self-dialogue is easier than you might think, but you will need to stick with it for several weeks to see best results. Here are a few ideas to get started:

- Go to a bookstore or go online and buy a book on meditation or a meditation audio CD. This is a great way to get started—especially if you are unconvinced that it will help you. Listening to a meditation CD nightly for four to six weeks will demonstrate how powerful this new tool for your mental well-being really is and you will be glad you did it. Remember to stick with it for a while to develop your abilities. The ability to easily meditate comes with practice and each attempt will allow you to cleanse your thoughts a little bit more easily each time.

- Take a course in meditation. There are numerous resources that will help you to learn this technique. Private businesses, educational institutions and even the YMCA may offer such courses. Take the class with a friend so you can discuss your results as you go through this experience.

- Set a time each day to commune with the memory of your wife. You can do this by closing your eyes and being silent for a few minutes, reflecting on what your wife might want you to tell her. With practice, you will be able to get into a deep reflective state quite easily in spite of surrounding distractions, even to the point that you could do this while sitting at your desk at work or waiting for an appointment.

- Ask your wife's guiding spirit to subconsciously provide you with the correct thoughts and influences on important decisions of the day. Allow yourself to feel her presence with you while you do daily activities like riding in the car listening to her favorite song. Think about things that remind you of her. This is your time to commune.

- Meditate on a central characteristic of your wife. This may be a reflection on a ritual that you often shared with that person, such as sharing a spa or lying in front of a fireplace on a cold winter night. Meditate on the topics you discussed, focusing on her voice, demeanor and what her presence felt like to you while you shared those moments together. Eventually, you should feel free to control the meditation to bring in new thoughts that are on your mind today, and lead the meditation through that issue. With practice, you should eventually feel that you can connect with the essence of your wife on any issue at hand.

Use your newly found skills for other needs such as health improvement, working relationships and other personal goals you wish to clarify and resolve in your mind.

I keep a motivating poem entitled "The Victor", which I was given during my time in that stressful job position, on my desk as a reminder of the power of one's beliefs. You might also want to place this poem in your workspace as a reminder to take time to tune out the world now and then, and tune into yourself. My favorite quatrain from it goes:

"The Victor"
C. W. Longenecker

Life's battles don't always go
To the stronger or faster man.
But sooner or later, the man who wins
Is the man who thinks he can.

Instructions:

1. Make a serious attempt to learn the skill of meditation. Use some of the suggestions mentioned above like reading about it, using guided audio CDs and by practicing daily. It takes time to learn the skill.
2. Practice meditating at the same time of day every day for a minimum of four weeks. It is not easy to shed all of the negative self-dialogue in a few sessions. It took months for the self-talk to get into your subconscious, so give yourself time to shed it as well. After four weeks, make a simple assessment of whether or not you are feeling better.
3. Lastly, if you are concerned by a potential religious conflict or a physical health concern, consult your religious leader or physician and get his or her opinion. You should find that he or she will be supportive of your desire to reduce stress and your desire to tune into your innermost thoughts.

Journaling follow-up:

1. How have I attempted to incorporate meditation into my daily routine?
2. How has meditation helped me work through negative self-talk and negative energy from my mind?
3. How does meditation allow me to cope with the sense of loss and focus on the love we shared for each other?

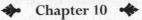

Chapter 10

Use
Affirmations

The death of one's wife seems to put the whole world into a state of doubt. Issues that were never previous concerns now become major worries that constantly preoccupy one's mind. We fear that we have lost control and that our situation is going to get worse. We wonder if our finances are going to be sufficient to live on; we worry that our children will no longer have the advantages that we wanted to provide them. The list goes on and on. Worrying about the future can create substantial barriers to our healing process, as this negative and unproductive energy drains us.

One of the best ways to stop this downward spiral of negative thinking is to reverse it through the use of affirmations. An affirmation is simply the assertion that something exists or is true. We have affirmations already that guide us every day when we subconsciously reaffirm our behavior in certain situations. An example would be, *There I go again, losing my car keys. I am so forgetful.* This subconsciously implants the undesirable trait that we do not have the ability to be organized. We label ourselves forgetful and expect future behaviors to be the same. We can also affirm a positive state of being by thinking to ourselves, *I can do this presentation well, because I know the sales data accurately reflects what the company should do.* This type of positive affirmation is a good example of how a person who desires confidence can easily improve his or her state of mind and perform well. Positive affirmation can dramatically improve the mindset of those who are grieving. Next, let's look at how to focus on eliminating negative affirmations and shift focus to affirmations that will yield positive results.

***

Changing your belief system

Men and women strive to maintain healthy senses of control over their lives. However, through the experience of losing spouses, they often feel a sense of helplessness in that "nothing in my life is within my control." Through the powerful efforts of affirmations, they can be enlightened to see the connection between embracing positive attitudes and thought patterns and their ultimate purpose in obtaining their life goals and improved senses of being. Men particularly find it challenging to move from their stereotypical and historically proven deliberate method of thinking toward one driven by changing their subconscious belief system. Making such a shift can help transform their lives from one of grief to one of hope by reaching beyond the comfort zone of what traditionally worked for them in the past.

***

First, we need to understand the power of affirmations and how they control our instinctive reactions. That is, an affirmation can cause us to behave in a certain way without even thinking about it. Affirmations become automatic. A simple affirmation that illustrates this is the belief that when you run a red light at a busy intersection, you have a high probability of suffering an accident and therefore an injury. Our belief in this assertion is so strong, because of the severity of the outcome. We stop at red lights without even thinking about putting our feet on the brake pedal. We are programmed to respond in that manner for our survival. What if we could affirm that our new lives without our spouses will be filled with success and happiness and have it so strongly believed, as in the stopping at red lights example, that it would become automatic within us? Our mindset throughout our daily routine will begin to support this belief and make it real. The feelings of success will steadily develop, and a positive outcome will prevail.

In affirming we basically program new beliefs into our subconscious from which our behaviors will follow to create our new reality. This is not some "Jedi mind trick" to fool us into false belief systems. By building on a foundation of affirmations concerning our core values and ultimate goals, our sense of being improves. However, if we do not define what those goals are, we will not develop new affirmations to center upon, so we will never change our present behavior. Hence, we will not obtain the goal.

There are many excellent resources (books, audio CDs, seminars and online coursework) on the power of affirmations, and I highly suggest you delve deeper into this subject. It can become a lifelong skill for use in all aspects of life. The intent here is to get you to make a real attempt at it, see some positive results and develop a new interest in building your skills from there.

Because of its dramatic results, I continue to use the power of affirmation every day of my life. Affirming has helped me become a better parent and a confident presenter in business meetings, and it improved other skill development areas in my life. One of the most significant effects was that affirmation allowed me to completely stop the need for taking a prescription medication for gastric reflux. During the period I had severe reflux symptoms, I was told by two doctors that I would need to take a drug for the rest of my life and that I could expect my condition to get worse as I grew older. I had lost a significant amount of weight and the condition persisted for over a year with no improvement. When I was told by a third doctor that the root cause of my reflux was due to stress, I realized and affirmed that my stressful perception of my job and its environment was not accurate. I replaced that belief with one of my health and welfare being my utmost concern. This is not to say that I affirmed that I no longer cared about my abilities on the job; I just affirmed that I didn't own problems (such as office politics) over which I had no control. This allowed my stress to decrease slowly and, over several months, my symptoms went away.

To begin utilizing affirmations, generate a written statement that describes a new, positive vision for an issue of concern. In beginning the affirmation process, you should have no more than five affirmations for five concern areas to get the best results. By focusing on these few issues, you will perceive the results faster and they will be more significant.

First, jot down five areas of concern. Define each problem and then rewrite it in a positive statement that describes a state of being wherein the problem has become a strength. For example, let's say that you have a concern that since your wife has died, your investments are in danger, because no one is closely managing their performance. An affirmation to remove this anxiety could be: *I am a resourceful person who can find a trustworthy financial advisor and establish a great relationship with him to help me make good, informed decisions about my investments.* Maybe you are concerned about being a good role model in parenting because your wife was more patient in child rearing. A possible affirmation statement could be: *I am a patient and loving parent who is a good role model for my children each and every day.*

Next, let's look at some sample concern areas and corresponding affirmations that you can use (you can also start by writing your own). Simple one-line sentence affirmations are easy to remember and infuse more quickly into your mind, but if a second sentence really helps to clarify the new behavior or mindset, then add it. Keep any affirmation for a particular concern area to no more than two sentences. Remember to write down these new affirmations in a way that reflects a positive state of being to reset your subconscious mind with the desired outcome:

Concern: Lack of confidence to carry on and be happy again without my wife.

Affirmation: Because of the love we shared, my wife would want me to carry on with my life and be happy in all that I do. Therefore, I am blessed knowing that I have experienced this depth of love that others may never enjoy.

Concern: There are just way too many things to do, and I can't do it all.

Affirmation: I can learn to change my daily routine and set up systems that help me to get things done or be satisfied that not all things need to be done immediately.

Write these affirmations down on a card and read them first thing in the morning and again before retiring to bed. If you can, try and read them sometime near the middle of the day for consistent exposure to these new beliefs. Ideally, the affirmations should be read several times throughout the day for the quickest, most dramatic results. Over time, when the affirmation slowly enters your subconscious mind through the frequent reading of the statement, you will begin to fashion your belief system. As your core belief system begins to change, you will begin to see small transformations in your behavior that support your affirmed future state of being. Typically, to see results you will be required to read your affirmations daily for four to six weeks.

***

"Marnie placed a magnet on our refrigerator that is a quote from Winston Churchill. It reads, 'Never, never, never give up!' She embodied that affirmation throughout her entire battle with cancer. After she passed away, I found some medical records that listed all of the chemotherapies and procedures she endured in our fight. I can't imagine what strength it must have taken to do what she did. I'm not so sure I would have been able to do it. But that saying is still on the refrigerator and reading it still gives me the motivation I need to continue on and to do my best for her. I don't want to disappoint her. That quote gives me all the kick in the pants I need to keep moving forward." –Ross

***

Instructions:

1. List five concern areas that are constantly recurring in your mind's self-talk and write them down expressing accurately your state of mind.
2. Rewrite each of the five concerns in a positive state of being where the statement reflects the original issue as a strength or the desired future condition. Use one or two sentences to describe this new strength area in a manner meaningful to you.
3. Write these five affirmations on a card or cards and locate them (wallet or pocket) where you can read them at least two or three times a day. These will be your five affirmations that you will seek to enact. Remember, for the best results, read your five affirmations when you first get up, during the day (lunch) and when you go to bed at night.
4. Practice reciting your affirmations daily for four to six weeks.
5. Note the results as you begin to change your behaviors and when you notice a specific change, recite the affirmation once again to cement that feeling and thought into your subconscious mind.
6. Obtain other resources for in-depth learning on the power of affirmations.

Journaling follow-up:

1. How have I utilized affirmations to help reprogram my belief system?
2. What specific positive affirmations have I found most helpful?
3. How have I noticed these affirmations affecting my thoughts and behaviors as I proceed with my life without my wife?

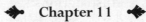 Chapter 11 ◆

Make and
Keep Friends

Many times when a death occurs, the surviving family receives countless offers of support from both people they know and sometimes from those whom only the deceased knew. Sometimes numerous family, friends and co-workers offer their support in a multitude of ways. If you feel this is true in your case and you are feeling alone in your grief, read on, as the purpose of this chapter is to get you to reach out and accept the help that you need.

Modern culture centers greatly around self-sufficiency. For many men, it is a sign of personal strength to refuse charity or offers of assistance. We are so embarrassed by offers of help that our responses are almost automatic: *No—don't worry about me, I'll be all right.* We have probably responded this way numerous times over a variety of circumstances.

No matter your response, the fact is that you are probably not all right. Your world has been turned upside down with your wife's death, questions are circulating in your mind and, to compound it all, you don't have a clue on how to get back on track. This is the time to take the help these caring souls are offering to you. There couldn't be a more practical and meaningful time to accept the help of others.

***
Getting by with a little help from my friends

When widows and widowers were asked what helped them best cope with grief, both men and women resoundingly reported support from family and friends. They stressed the importance of having someone to talk to about their grief and their memories of the deceased. However, widowers reported that it was valuable to them if friends be patient while they worked through their grief and not expect their pain to be resolved in a finite period of time. Some widowers discussed the benefit of receiving physical and emotional assistance from friends. Several widowers in Tom's grief support group noted they are not "naturally chatty" and do not ask for help easily. They recognize that people have lives of their own and cannot always be as supportive as they wish because of their own time, financial, and emotional commitments. Knowing another grieving widower to share thoughts was also helpful in the journey from grief to healing.

***

Accepting help will not only ease your many burdens, it will also let your friends cope with the loss as well. Many of these people want to honor the memory of your wife and pay a tribute by doing something nice for the loved ones she left behind. Friends, family and co-workers can feel a deeper sense of connectedness to your wife through helping the family of the deceased.

Offers of help will come in many forms. Employers and counseling center staff may call to check on how you are coping with your adjustments to daily tasks and emotional well-being. Friends may bring you home-cooked meals, provide transportation or visit you to talk. You will hear offers such as, "If you need anything, anything at all, just call me." Well, go ahead and make that call; you'll be glad you did.

During Terri's final months and, after her death, I began having lunch with Steve, a former co-worker of mine who had also lost his wife to cancer at an early age. This friendship was very valuable, because I felt he was the only person who really understood what I was feeling. I told him about my anger and the sense of unfairness of it all among other emotions that coursed through me. I was able to share very personal thoughts with him, as others would not have been able to understand and console me in the same way as he did. Steve was a bright lighthouse in the storm that was tossing me around. He was proof that living beyond a wife's death was not only survivable, but would also take time.

I also accepted several gracious offers to share dinners at friends' homes with their families. My first reaction was to refuse these intrusions into their lives, because I felt a strong urge to prove to myself and my sons that I could quickly adjust and straighten this mixed-up world that we lived in. I did not want to let anyone down nor have the person possibly think that I couldn't manage my life. Looking back, I now see how foolish it was to think being independent was of such high importance to me at the most tumultuous time in my life. Eventually, I realized that I needed breaks from the stress of something as simple as planning a home-cooked meal, so I accepted. These dinners afforded me time to relax and to talk to good people about what was going on in my life. Just being able to talk and hear a few encouraging words was enough to get me through trying days. Those dinners were very meaningful to my family.

Consider the next examples where you can accept help from others:
- Call a person you know who has lost his or her spouse and ask the person if it is alright to discuss what he or she learned from the experiences. Just talking and sharing about each other's experiences will give you a sense that you are not alone, that others have survived their losses and so you can, too!
- Accept an offer to go out to dinner or host a dinner at your home. If someone offers to drop off a prepared meal, tell the person that you will only accept it if that person will share it with you over good conversation. Talking with the individual will be more rewarding and beneficial to both of you, so take every opportunity you can.
- Go to the movies or a live theatrical performance with a friend and pick one that your wife might have enjoyed. Conversation to

and from the theater could center on what favorite types of performances you enjoyed with your wife.

- Take an offer for free childcare so that you can "catch up" on errands not easily done with small children in tow.

***

"Ray is this big, burly guy I know who runs a bar and he is your stereotypical tough guy, long beard—the works. Two days after Barb died, after this big snow storm, Ray came over and started snowplowing my driveway. I went outside to say thanks, and he told me to go back inside and get him a cup of coffee with a few expletives to motivate me to be quick about it. Then, he came inside the house and, after having a couple of cups of coffee, he pretty much demanded I join him to go snowplowing. I spent about four hours with Ray that day and it was time away from the grief that I really needed. Here was a guy who had no reason to help me, because I never really patronized his place, but he still came over to help. That's a guy with a big heart." –Mike

***

When you accept help, whether from a professional or a friend, you will be staying connected to the support base of the people who want to see you make a successful transition through your grieving process. Your interaction with them will strengthen your emotional health and give you numerous solutions to large issues looming over you at this time. You may not get the exact result that you would have gotten if you alone had completed the task or you may get a result better than expected. Don't fret about these details; just take satisfaction that the help lifted you a little higher out of this dark hole of depression and know that you're climbing out of it.

Instructions:

1. Try any or all of the ideas mentioned. Sometimes you might just have to force yourself to reach out and call someone to give yourself a break from the grind of resetting your life. Pick an idea and make the call.

2. Make a point to accept any offer of help from someone. When a person asks if there is anything they can do to help you, say "yes."

3. For those special people who reach out to you with a special invitation, accept it and then send them a "thank you" to express how meaningful it was to you to have their friendship and to have spent that time together.

Journaling follow-up:

1. What has been one example during this past week when I accepted help from a friend?

2. How has my ability to accept help from this friend affected my relationship with him or her?

3. What opportunities have my friends and I had to reflect on my wife's memories, and how have these opportunities allowed us to provide mutual support to one another in our grieving processes?

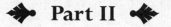 Part II

Healing
From Within

"What lies behind us and what lies before us are tiny matters
compared to what lies within us."
Ralph Waldo Emerson

Chapter 12

Construct a
Memory Box

Many people collect items that have little to no significant value to others. Terri created a collection of teddy bears to share in the merriment when our boys were smitten with these furry friends. These were especially fun for Terri to collect, because one of her college roommates had given her the nickname of "Teddy." That name stuck with Terri long after her college days were over. Some collections are more formal, as in a coin or stamp collection, and others are informal. We have collections of golf balls, jewelry, tools, books and crafted items, to name a few. If we look around our living space, we see in every corner of every room items that define who we are, what we value and where we have been.

When your wife passes on, these objects she leaves behind instantly become of great value to you. These inanimate objects symbolize a fragment of who she was in life. She found enjoyment in possessing these objects, and now suddenly, you see that enjoyment for yourself, because these belongings are all you have to hold onto besides your memories of her. A favorite record album or purse begins to take on a new significance, although before you would not have thought twice about its intrinsic value. By acknowledging the object's value to your spouse, you begin to really understand her core values and being. You probe deeper into what brought her the simple pleasures of life.

Security Guard

Hence, these objects that define the key characteristics of her life now become priceless to her family. Men and women alike place priceless value on material objects, which represent the core essences of who their spouses were to them. Soon after his wife's death, a widower may experience an intense sense of fear of losing these everyday objects that he holds in high value but others may not. Widowers fear that by not retaining these valuable objects, they risk gradual loss of the core value of who their spouses were to them. This fear of losing or misplacing these valued objects drives widowers to find a safe place where they can be secured.

Thus, if you are to capture the sheer essence of her spirit after she is gone, a simple way to begin is by cherishing the objects that partially defined her by collecting a few and saving them for your posterity. You can keep them safe by placing them in a secure place or memory box.

Immediately after Terri's death, returning to work seemed pointless to me. I had to take time to readjust to my new life without her and complete many of the tasks in this book (such as the logistics items described in chapter 2) to get my ship righted again. As a release from the stress, and because I feared I would lose some of Terri's memories, the boys and I built three hope chests to place at the foot of our beds. Woodworking is a hobby of mine, so I had the tools and skill to do this project well. The project was a huge stress reliever for me in that it was a "time-out" from thinking all about the logistical issues I still needed to resolve. Sanding a piece of hard maple can be very therapeutic. We placed many of the "valuables" that described Terri in those hope chests. In my memory box, I included items of extreme value to me such as the scrapbook from chapter 13, photos of Terri, our wedding album, love letters and a cross she used for prayer in her final days. In the event of a house fire, that box will be first to go out the window even before the insurance policies!

With these valuables secured in that hope chest, I felt much better knowing that I had a primary location for the most important items that described Terri and the life I shared with her. I no longer fear losing or misplacing small things that have meaning to our life together. In fact, that box is of such importance to me that I now also use it to hold other things of great value.

***

"One of the most precious possessions that I have of Donna is a pair of glasses that she just fell in love with and bought at a rummage sale. But Donna had me customize them with some small decorative rhinestones on the bows—it cost me twenty-five dollars on a pair of frames that cost her a quarter! But to me, those glasses are priceless now." Larry

***

You do not need woodworking skills, nor do you need to build a hope chest. You can make your memory box whatever you wish it to be. This "box" to store treasured items can be a framed collection, a shadow box, a hope chest or even a simple cigar box. Ask around for other ideas and even consider inviting a friend over who is handy with tools to help create your memory box. You can also refer to chapter 6, "Get Help!", in which you can enroll the help of a professional. By keeping a few of these cherished items in a safe place, you can rest assured knowing that a few tokens of your wife's life will be there to browse through on anniversary dates or similar meaningful times on the calendar.

***

"Marnie was incredibly organized. She started these storage bins for each of our three sons. In them, she stored schoolwork, photos and anything that she thought would be valued at some later time and place. There are certainly items in there that are keepsakes of her. I am really glad she created such an easy way to hold onto these memories for my boys. I continue to add to each sons' "memory box" as she would have done. Heck, I even discovered that she had a box just for the two of us and in it is some stuff that is *not* to be shared with the boys!" –Ross

***

Instructions:

1. If your wife had a collection, but did not formally display it, think of a way to display these objects in a manner that pays tribute to her passion. This may mean a display case, a frame or other means to show off these precious items.
2. You may want to create a true memory box containing an assortment of her possessions. Such boxes can be easily made or purchased from a craft store or a furniture store. Things that you might include are:
   a. Personal effects–watches, a hair brush, items from her purse, bill-fold, etc.
   b. Favorite books–her journal, a scrapbook (see chapter 13).
   c. Diplomas, awards, trophies, service medals, etc.

Journaling follow-up:

1. What items do I feel were cherished by my wife and I, and what type of memory box would be meaningful for me to create?
2. What emotions have I been feeling about my wife as I create the memory box, and why have I been feeling these emotions?
3. How has the act of creating this memory box helped me to gain a greater understanding of her simple pleasures of life and values she held?

♦ Chapter 13 ♦

Gather a
Scrapbook

Many people write in a diary or journal to chronicle their experiences for future review of their thoughts. Perhaps your deceased wife didn't document her thoughts in this way, but collected printed materials, photos or trinkets from special events in your family members' lives such as graduations, family vacations or special celebrations.

When we rediscover this memorabilia after our wives' deaths, it puts smiles on our faces, because it reminds us of happier times in our pasts.

As we look through these things, we think of those times we spent with our lost loved ones. We may never know the origin of some items or how they came to stay in the possession of our spouses, but because they were never thrown out, we know that our spouses felt they were worth keeping. These trinkets of their pasts meant something to them and hence are a tangible piece of the history of the lives we spent with them as well.

The goal of this exercise is to create a different art form in which you can "write" the pages of the "diary" of your spouse, even though she may never have formally written one. This art form diary will beautify the life of your wife, because it is a scrapbook that utilizes items she herself collected. A scrapbook is a great way to honor the memory of your wife, because it uses items directly from her daily life and preserves them for future reference. If we do not make an effort to create such a catalogue, many of their facets will be forgotten. Organizing these scraps of our lives in a book can bring back memories of happiness and times well spent together. The book should be much more than a mere photo album. Pictures may speak a thousand words, but other objects may do just the same and be included in such a meaningful book.

***

Where's the Owner's Manual?

Men can derive a comforting sense of nostalgia toward past memories with their spouses by creating scrapbooks. Men are usually not wired to be organized nor attend to detail, particularly when that activity involves another trustworthy person to coordinate. However, with the loss of a wife, men have a new need to regain control over documenting details of family life. Scrapbooking or any other means of organizing life's events in a readily accessible fashion fulfills this new need. Men do find this deliberate activity extremely healing as it classifies tangible items in an organized and readily accessible format which cements the qualities that they value in their spouses and in their relationship.

***

One of the best places that I found materials to use in my scrapbook came from Terri's purse. Her purse held a lot of defining items that I will always reflect upon as symbols of what she did for me and the boys. She kept our whole family in check with a family events calendar, the always present pack of gum to satisfy a sudden urge in church, even those mixed drink sword skewers that the boys always wanted to have Mom keep for them. I completed the scrapbook, because I felt a strong need to document the small stuff in our lives that I was already missing soon after Terri's passing.

After I completed my scrapbook, I wanted to ensure nothing could ever fall out of it and I wanted something to protect the exterior cover. I quickly realized that a cloth bag would be just the perfect thing to protect this cherished book. The answer literally fell into my lap as I reorganized our closet. I found that the perfect bag to use was the bag that stored Terri's favorite designer purse. It couldn't have been more fitting. In a strange way, that bag still functioned as a purse containing all those items she held for our family.

It is very easy to create a scrapbook. Visit your local craft store to get started with some basic materials. Since scrapbooking is a very popular hobby today, you should have no trouble finding supplies or even ideas from such a store. To get ideas for what might go into the book, check your wife's purse, wallet, car or even her desk at work. You can include membership cards, pins, ticket stubs and, of course, the much outdated photos she carried of you and the family. Your scrapbook can also include journal segments that you have written, which can help explain the items glued onto the pages. If your wife had a bag of sorts (a gym bag, favorite pillowcase, briefcase, etc.) you may wish to store it within that case as a further means of remembrance.

If you feel you do not have the artistic skills to create a scrapbook that will be acceptable to you, ask for help. There are many people who are involved in this hobby and can do a very good job for you. They can be found at work, through your network of friends and family or even a visit to a craft store can lead you to the right person. You can have them teach you this skill while you create the project or you can contract them to do it for you with minimal help.

***

"My teenage daughter put a scrapbook together and kept a diary throughout our battle. It is a private book for her that she keeps as an uplifting memory of her mom. Because Mickey was diagnosed when my daughter was just ten, for her there are few memories of the happier times we had as a family. But the book really illustrates that there were happier times and our life wasn't just about the darkness we endured. Without a doubt, I think putting that book together really helped her grieve. She was encouraged to express the love she has for her mother in her own way and it was a natural fit for her since she is a more shy type of person." –Mark

***

Once your scrapbook is completed, you may wish to store it in the Memory Box (see chapter 12) to preserve its importance to you. When an anniversary or birthday comes around and you feel the need to reflect upon and honor your wife, the scrapbook can easily be located and reviewed in a very meaningful way. The book can be shared with others who may also be experiencing a great sense of loss.

Instructions:

1. Peruse your wife's living space where she may have stored memorable items. Look in every room of the home, as you will be surprised where she might have stored objects of importance. This includes areas such as where the laundry was done, a study or family room. Collect items that you feel describe the person to you. You may find items such as extra photos that you may wish to give away to family and friends during this activity.

2. Visit a craft store and ask about scrapbooking supplies to get an idea of what materials are available to develop your scrapbook. You might want to mention items that you found that may have special scrapbooking needs, like old and fragile photos or yellowed newspaper clips, so that you can ask the best way to preserve them. You may even want to ask about classes to help you assemble the book and give you a reason to get out and meet other people. Many craft stores offer such classes or can direct you as to where to go for assistance.

3. Make your scrapbook and enjoy the fact that you laid another stone in the monument of your loved one's memory.

Journaling follow-up:

1. What mementos of my wife have I assembled in an organized display that truly represents important aspects of her life?

2. What did I feel about the relationship we shared as I created various portions of the scrapbook?

3. How will the scrapbook allow me to reflect upon the memories of the special times we shared together?

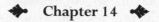

Chapter 14

Cherish
Personal Effects

After the death of a wife, one is left with the particularly painful decision of what to do with her jewelry. Many women have a wide variety of jewelry such as bracelets, watches, necklaces and earrings. Jewelry may have a higher personal value than anything else a wife may have owned, in monetary value and, of course, in sentimental value. Therefore, the surviving members of the family may cherish these items over all other belongings. This makes the disposition of these items very important, and a high potential for problems exists if the items are not disbursed in a fair fashion. Surviving members can either be comforted or offended by the way these cherished items are bequeathed. Now the question becomes how to handle it all in such a way that abides by her wishes, but also in a way that is fair to her inheritors.

Ideally, your late wife specified what was to be done with these articles before she passed on. Hopefully, she either stated in her will or wrote down in her own hand precisely what should be given to whom. If your wife specified each item by leaving a handwritten note, then it might be a good idea to give this note to the inheritor. This personalizes the gift, as well as removes doubt that this decision was specifically desired by your wife. This also leaves no room for argument with the surviving member who enacted her wishes.

Unfortunately, many times it isn't possible to have this pre-work completed. In such cases, here are some suggestions.

The disbursement of wedding bands likely becomes the most difficult decision to make. All sorts of ideas race through one's mind, along with suggestions from her family members. Some will say a female of the family should get the woman's band, even if it means diverting the band laterally in the family tree, thereby skipping over the children of the woman.

This was a particular issue in my wife's family where they didn't understand how a woman's wedding ring could be given to sons. With no daughter to whom to pass Terri's ring, compounded by the strong desire to give our sons a symbol of our marriage vows and the love we held for each other, Terri and I jointly created the solution. When I speak of this concept to others, they are truly amazed at the significance of such a symbol. We decided to take our wedding rings, the diamonds they contained and the two necklaces that I had given Terri when she gave birth to each of my sons and had them melted down and transformed into three new rings: one for each of my sons and one for me. The result created a new symbol of the love Terri and I shared and the importance of our sons' births, so that for the rest of our lives we would have that symbol close to us. There is never a day where I don't look down at that ring and remember what a true blessing she was in our lives. Later, my ring played an important part in remaining connected to Terri's memory, which I further describe in chapter 29, "Imagine the Other Side."

There are many other ways to fairly divide jewelry. However, I believe asking relatives for their help may end up being counterproductive unless there is someone who was particularly close to your wife, who is respected by the remaining members of the family and who can manage such an important disbursement process well. Even so, there may be a high risk of alienating a family member.

***

I Did It My Way
You—and only you—should decide what is to be done with your wife's personal belongings. Don't force yourself to go through these things until you are ready—take your time. Early in grief, you may not have the energy

or desire to do anything with them. Remember that some people may try to speed up your healing by advising you to quickly do something with her belongings. Don't let others make decisions for you. It is not detrimental to leave your spouse's belongings right where they are for now. When you have the energy to go through them, you will. Do it only when the time feels right for you.

When you are ready, go through your wife's personal items. You may find it hard to give away these belongings. Instead of parting with everything at once, you might make three groups of items: one to keep, one to give away and one to be labeled "not sure." Ask your children for help. Take a look at how other widowers and their families met their needs of distributing their deceased wives' belongings.

Here is one example of how widower Jerry B. did so in a very systematic way:

"About a month after Gloria passed away, I invited the family over to the house to split up her jewelry. There was no way I was going to let it just sit in the box. To be fair, I picked a number and the closest one to my number picked an item first, then the others took their respective turns. After the first round, we reversed the picking order. We did this until all of the jewelry was gone. For me to leave her jewelry in a box and not let it be enjoyed by her family would be crazy." —Jerry B.

***

One consideration that will eliminate all of these concerns is the idea to transform key jewelry into completely new pieces for each of your wife's inheritors. Custom jewelers are set up to make a variety of pieces and styles that can live on in a new shape and still signify the significance of the materials. The precious metals of the jewelry can be melted down and split amongst the desired inheritors. The precious gemstones can be split and allocated in a similar fashion. Items can range from new rings and necklaces, to less costly items such as tie tacks. Even if there is not an over abundance of jewelry to convert, a single stone can be mounted in an existing cross necklace, for example, to memorialize the person with her most significant possession.

Instructions:

1. Assemble the pieces of jewelry that were of significant meaning to your wife. Take them to a jeweler and discuss how the pieces can be transformed into new pieces for gifting to the inheritors.
2. In the event that your wife possessed a limited collection of jewelry to choose from, collect favorite items that helped to define her life and ask a custom jeweler for helpful ideas.

Journaling follow-up:

1. What specific pieces of jewelry do I want to ensure will bring the best intrinsic value to the recipients in an equitable manner so that they can reflect on their significant memories of my wife? What items do I wish to retain for myself?
2. What are the struggles or concerns I am facing as I attempt to face decisions about what to do with my wife's jewelry?
3. How did disbursing my wife's most valued keepsakes help me and others reflect on her memory?

◆ Chapter 15 ◆

Wear Me,
Feel Me

When our spouses pass away, the void that remains engrosses our
every day. With every room that we walk into and every task we
do without them, we are constantly reminded that they are gone from
our physical world. We are reminded over and over that we will never
again have that sense of being physically connected to them. We long to
feel their presences in our beds, to look in their eyes across a dinner table,
to smell their perfume or to just feel one last hug from them. We can
reflect on vivid memories to fill our minds with positive thoughts about
them, but the physical contact of this strong and loving relationship has
been sharply cut off. There is no one thing or person that can replace the
intimacy that we experienced and then had so quickly taken away from
us. In the immediate weeks following the death, the loss of intimacy is felt
very strongly because of the sudden end of physical connection.

However, we can draw closer to their memory by connecting to the
clothing that they used to help define their profession, character, hobbies
and even what gave them comfort while lounging around the house. Our
clothing is an extension of our persona. The feeling one gets by putting
on a pair of well worn blue jeans after a week of wearing three piece suits
is hard to describe!

If we really think about it: What is it that gives us this comforting feeling? After all, a pair of jeans is just woven cotton, not significantly different from the material of which many casual dress slacks are made. I suggest that these comforting clothes are much more than their softness, fit or worn and tattered appearance. They symbolize by appearance alone that when you are wearing this item, you are a different person. I have found these clothes are a release of sorts. I am not working, but enjoying myself in this moment because I am wearing my relaxation clothing or my "go out and have a fun" clothing. They clearly state that I am in a different environment now, and I want my clothing to match what I am feeling. Our clothing can clearly change our state of mind and make us feel better.

***

Macho Man?

Men and women in grief report similar struggles with the devastating sense of loneliness and emptiness as they face the loss of intimacy and companionship due to the death of their spouses. When all is said and done, men realize their macho, outward demeanor cannot replace their human need for intimacy. The opportunity to identify and create their loved one's meaningful piece of clothing into a renewed sense of comfort and connection will provide moments of relief from periods of despair and loneliness.

***

That same comforting feeling that your favorite pair of jeans or a favorite T-shirt gives you can also be achieved with an article of clothing your wife once used. By browsing through her wardrobe, you can find many examples of defining items that can be used to memorialize her life. While chapter 37 describes the benefits that come from donating your lost love's clothing, this chapter explains how to hang onto a few items and convert them into a long lasting and comforting memorial.

A good friend of Terri's handcrafted a beautiful quilt for her that Terri used religiously while watching television. I know it gave her great comfort because she used it often. Because she loved this quilt so much, it now gives me a special feeling each and every time I use it.

You might be wondering how you could possibly use some article of clothing that your wife enjoyed. After all, you might harbor reservations about wearing clothes that are not yours. Maybe you find that your wife's clothes are just too big or too small for your everyday use. Regardless, do not lose sight of the fact that others are grieving their own loss as well. Consider that a younger member of the family might be comforted by your offering it as a gift. My youngest son, who always seems to think the house is far too cold at night for sleeping comfortably, will reach for a pair of Terri's favorite flannel pajamas, in spite of having flannel pajamas of his own, when the temperature drops into single digits. There may be a bonus to it fitting them perfectly! They may also have thought about this idea, but maybe they were reluctant to ask, being sensitive to only your needs. This is a great opportunity to comfort others, as well as yourself, and to honor your loved one's memory in the process, so why not give it a try?

***

"I met Kathy through her cousin whom I knew from high school. One time before we were married, I got to know Kathy a little bit better when we all stayed on Chamber's Island at a place where she and her cousin worked during the summer. Because I was assigned to sleep on the couch, Kathy gave me her "Bambi Blanket" to keep warm that night. I didn't know at the time that it was a childhood keepsake of hers. However, many years later she told me from that day forward, she knew we were going to be together. To this day, every time I use that blanket, it instantly works to keep her memory alive in me. It's priceless." –Rick

***

Here are a couple of suggestions as to the potential this idea may hold for you and others:

- **A throw blanket:** Your wife's favorite throw that she may have frequently used while watching television may provide comfort to you while you watch your favorite show. You may never have felt the need to use a throw blanket to keep yourself cozy, but your wife may have felt this way. A technique to draw you nearer to her memory of the blanket may be to lower the thermostat a bit to physically feel why she appreciated it so much.

- **Her gloves:** Even a woman's set of gloves could be used as a way to remember her. Use the gloves as a case for an extra set of sunglasses or pens & pencils in your car. They can help prevent scratches on your sunglasses or keep pens and pencils from falling to the bottom of the glove box. It will be soothing knowing that every time you reach for a pen from that glove, you will think of her.
- **Her winter scarf:** Many scarves are of a design and versatile color scheme that men can easily use them.
- **Her favorite team cap:** Today, sport team colors are worn by everyone. Use a cap for those times when you didn't take a shower and you have bed head but you need to run that errand.
- **Her handkerchief:** Put a handkerchief sprayed with your wife's favorite perfume in your briefcase to remind you of her presence. Each time you reach for your keys or coins, you will smell that her essence is near you.

Take a moment and say a short remembrance prayer or statement to your wife each time you reach for one of these personal belongings she enjoyed so much. It will help you retain a connection to her memory. The simple act of using a favorite item of hers will provide a small but meaningful level of comfort because you will now more fully appreciate the value she held for it. There are many ways that an object your wife used can serve a new and useful purpose for you. Be creative.

Instructions:

1. Try one of the ideas mentioned or be creative and try something different as a way to connect your wife's wardrobe with your or your family's memory of them.

Journaling follow-up:

1. What are a few of my wife's special items of clothing that provide me a special feeling of comfort?
2. What was my emotional reaction as I was browsing through my wife's wardrobe, searching for these items?
3. What are some of the special memories that I have recalled as I use my wife's clothing as comfort?

✦ Chapter 16 ✦

Act Carefree
as a Child

If someone was to come up to you right now and say, "Tell me about the fondest times you had with your wife, and describe the mood that you both were in at the moment," what would your answer be? What feeling did this time with your wife impart on you? The past memories that people recall most fondly are those that put smiles on their faces. Feelings of cheerful fun and carefree happiness come to mind. Such playful antics, humorous situations, love-based teasing and dependable companionship often can be equated to childhood experiences.

Children want to have fun and share it with everyone around them. Many times, their desire for playfulness is a top priority. They can be in tears at one moment, but then quickly bounce back to their normal cheerfulness. Happiness is their goal; there is no need to fixate on work and distress. When work is to be done (and a child is committed to completing it!), children find creative ways to accomplish tasks with a positive spirit. For example, they might very well sing or whistle a tune while doing a household chore. Children often do not even realize they are doing it. Recall moments of happiness with your wife and ask yourself, did I not feel more childlike during those experiences?

Children also live in the moment. Except for extreme situations when their basic needs are threatened, they demonstrate very little sense of worry about the future. The future is something to deal with when the time comes. When spending happier days with your wife, time stood still. The togetherness was a means to feel secure in what the future might bring. Two people are more resilient than one. When we live in the moment, it allows us to free our minds from contemplating the future, which we cannot control. Living in the now affords us the mind space to strengthen the foundation of our relationships. Strong relationships precipitate happiness. When we are in a state of happiness, our worries fade and we become carefree. That sense of being carefree and being focused on your wife is what lives on in your heart today.

Children are usually more self assured than adults. They are far less concerned about competition and seeking approvals from peers. They move forward in their own belief sets and rarely worry about what peers may say to them. In fact, children go out of their way to enroll others in what they are experiencing. They seek out interaction or play time to be with others with the key objective of having fun. They genuinely want to be part of a group and want to experience the entire group having fun. A child's self-doubt comes when it stems from others who make a point to put them down. Letting go of the competition that surrounds us and becoming more secure with what we currently possess releases us from the stress of thinking selfishly and allows for more opportunity to focus on developing our own inner self.

I believe the best times with your wife were supported by three characteristics that children exhibit every day. These best times helped to make your life more full and rewarding in a loving relationship. These sensations of happiness, living in the moment and caring for others made all the difference in feeling alive. However, the ideas that once brought us such joy seem lost forever when our spouses die. The important point here is to know that the feelings that you once felt are still really there, they just are simply buried deep in your memories. And by recalling this sense of being fully alive, these feelings will endure as a gift your wife has given you.

***

Game Time

Men historically have spent less time raising and interacting with their children in their early years than their wives. Careers and other conflicting priorities only resulted in loss of experience in regards to truly becoming connected with their children's need for many men. Many widowers find themselves thrust into making significant changes in how they relate to children. By reflecting upon the childlike times spent with their spouses, widowers can rediscover the value of fun. Then through renewed efforts to engage in playful activities with children, men in grief find a gradual return of happiness. And maybe most significantly, by providing opportunities for children to feel a sense of normalcy again, this adds a much needed element to the healing process for the entire family.

***

When I think about how these feelings manifested in my relationship with Terri, I am comforted by those memories. I can immediately think of Terri's spirit, joy, laughter and the sense of caring she had for me, my sons and the people around her. One of Terri's greatest attributes was her ability to listen and her genuine interest in understanding those around her. Her character reverberated servitude to others framed in a state of happiness. I think being an elementary school teacher benefited Terri by allowing her to hang onto those attributes. Her work environment was much different from the corporate world I lived in. However, over my career, I learned that even in my highly competitive environment, when I acted in servitude to others and focused on a happier state of being, my days were more rewarding for me as well as my co-workers. I could do more with the willing aid of others and have myself and the people around me feeling better for it when my spirit was servitude framed in happiness.

In your grief, you may have forgotten the framework in which happier times existed. At best, you have lost the frequency of the laughing, hugging, sharing and giving of each other—the intrinsic rewards you used to enjoy in your togetherness. By framing the memory of your wife in the character of a child, it can help to relight the spirit from long ago that held your deepest conviction for her.

The activities in this chapter will help to push you into getting back into the childlike state of mind! Refresh your memory of being more childlike and look for happiness, living in the moment and caring for others. This will resurrect some of the best memories your wife gave you, the ones which made you feel alive.

***

"The challenges of trying to keep a house running smoothly with three young boys after losing my wife, Marnie, are sometimes overwhelming. I wonder sometimes if I'll ever see their shoes organized by the door without me having to ask them to do it. As frustrating as these things can be, I have to remind myself that they are children and they deserve to live as other children would live (that is, without so many responsibilities thrown onto their shoulders). My desire to give them that childhood back again manifested in an ice rink I built for them in our backyard. The time we spend on that rink playing hockey is the quality time we need of each other. I feel that by spending this time playing with them, they are a little bit closer to having more of a normal childhood. It also keeps me in check that sometimes shoes strewn about the floor is not that important." –Ross

***

It's time to start having fun again and feeling childlike cheerfulness by trying a few of the ideas mentioned next. You can add any message you like to these suggestions or maybe offer no message and feel secure in the reasoning behind why you did this task.

- Next time while checking out at a register in a grocery store, gas station or similar business, seek out a line in which a child is waiting with his or her parent. Ask the child's guardian for permission to buy a candy bar or other candy item for the child. Do this for the simple pleasure of seeing the child's reaction of happiness. Look at the child's smile and immediate shift in joy. Take notice of the guardian's reaction as well——it is sure to brighten the person's day, too!
- Purchase a new baby gift (any small baby item will do) and bring it to a hospital for a new couple's baby. You may want to write a

small card that you are gifting it in memory of your wife who had a childlike spirit. A great day to give this gift to a newborn is one who shares the same birthday with your wife. What a great way to remember your wife's birthday, by brightening the same day for some new parents!

- Purchase an item from a child who is doing a fundraiser. Your message to them may be that you remember someone who, like them, did a great job in her work and wish the child success in his or her fundraising.

- Volunteer for an organization that supports children. Maybe this could reflect your own past participation in a group like the Boy or Girl Scouts, Boys & Girls Club, etc. By doing so, you will experience firsthand fun and excitement to rekindle your spirit.

***

"I really think my relationship with my grandsons has changed since losing Marge—it's much closer now. I think we all have grown equally from this experience. We took a three-week trip to California and looked at so many rocks in Zion National Park that we joke about it today saying, 'How many rocks can a guy look at? Can we go now?' We spend so much time together that sometimes I have to tell them to go play with their buddies and not hang around an old guy like me. Deep down, our understanding of the little things in life is what's important." –Joe

***

Instructions:

1. Try one of the ideas listed at the end of this chapter or create one of your own that forms a connection to a child. Remember that the intent of this activity is to experience what children naturally seem to exuberate: happiness, living in the present and a sense of caring for others.

Journaling follow-up:

1. What is an activity I recently completed that helped me connect with a child?
2. How did this activity make me feel as I reflect on my own reaction, in addition to the child's/guardian's reaction?
3. Did this moment help me reflect on similar attributes and memories when my wife and I had a childlike experience? If so, what were they?

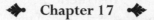

Chapter 17

Write a
Love Letter

What are love letters and why do we write them? They take on various formats from famous poems and novels to small playful notes in a lunch bag. The rationale most people would probably give for writing such a letter is that we have strong emotional attraction towards a person, but are too embarrassed to share these thoughts of the heart face to face. To be clearer about it, we write because we are *afraid* of how the other person might respond to us in person. We fear being laughed at, rejected, misunderstood or even getting no reaction at all. When we write our confidence is higher and we take more risk in detailing our true feelings than if we were to speak of the subject. Still, sometimes our self-consciousness interferes with truly communicating how we feel about a person, so we take the easy road and don't write at all. We *assume* they know how we feel about them. After all, why wouldn't they understand us? We married each other—right? We endlessly justify the reasoning for *not* doing it, but we do not think about the justification *for* doing it!

Stop and think for a moment what a terrible thing it is for a couple to assume their feelings of love for each other! Sharing one's genuine love in a clear, powerful message, unburdened by our self-consciousness, is the greatest gift we have for one another.

When the loss of a wife occurs, one of the most recurring and dis-comforting thoughts that a widower has is that he wishes he would have more completely communicated the magnitude of his love for his wife. Even in the best relationships, a love letter has the power of affirming to the beloved that there is no taking the relationship for granted.

***

Take Good Notes

Historically, men have been less inclined to engage in romance or sharing their deep-seated emotions toward their significant others via written form. Their myopic focus in life has typically been one of providing for the needs of others. Men falsely assume that by being a good provider, this alone demonstrates their love to a woman. But women need to hear that they are loved in addition to receiving the necessities of life. After death, this realization can be disturbing to a widower, particularly if he was not communicative in the relationship in this regard. In the midst of a man's grief, the bombardment of daily responsibilities makes the opportunity to reflect upon the relationship he experienced with his wife even more challenging, thereby adding to stress and therefore slowing the healing process.

Men who take the time to embrace the opportunity to examine their feelings of love for their spouses via written form experience a deeper sense of connection of the love they shared with their spouses.

***

As I look back on my relationship with Terri, I feel one of the most significant times I spent with her was at a Marriage Encounter weekend. It was during this retreat that we truly learned the value of communicating our deepest thoughts to each other in written form. Marriage Encounter is a program for married couples who are looking to strengthen their bonds to each other through a focused set of activities and reflection. When I first heard about it, I dismissed the program as something only for troubled marriages. I actually felt a bit insulted that my co-worker would suggest it to me. I couldn't have been more wrong.

At the training, we were amazed at how the simple tool of writing love letters to each other could be so powerful. We learned to journal the love, hopes and fears we held in our hearts. Everything was fair game. We did the weekend in the seventh year of our marriage and used it routinely for the remaining thirteen years together. Each anniversary card or birthday card or even a note after a passionate argument was an opportunity to "put it out there" in an honest forum so as not to be assuming of the other.

The love letters we shared throughout our marriage always made it possible to communicate regardless of the strong emotions that may have been behind them. In the end, in the course of Terri dying, it was with this journaling of love letters back and forth that we were able to communicate the difficult issues such as remarriage, parenting methods for the boys, life after death and dissemination of her personal belongings. I know we held "discussions" in this forum of exchanging letters that couples married fifty years might not ever experience. We felt deeply connected through the written word even though we often couldn't speak after reading the latest response. The journal of these thoughts we shared was ultimately cremated with her body to forever seal the significance they held for us. This feeling of connection to Terri continues as I write this book.

Writing forces the mind to shift from the day's distractions and gives us pause to focus on what we wish to clearly communicate. It allows for reflection to the purpose of our message and the opportunity to fully develop the clarity of it. It further preserves our thoughts in a permanent form for the benefit of revisiting the message at a later time. Because of these benefits to writing, I believe the written word carries more quality and therefore significance to the message than one of conversation. All too often the spoken word can be misconstrued as to the true meaning and modified in one's own mind as to what was heard versus actually said. Writing greatly diminishes these risks.

While it is no longer possible to physically express your love in the same manner, there are still ways to communicate love to your wife while bringing your spirit alive. Here are two activities you can do to reflect upon the love you shared with your wife and memorialize her contribution to your life:

- **Write a love letter:** Take out a sheet of paper and use this sentence as a kick-start to write a love letter to your wife: "When I think about you, I think of the many different ways you have shown love to me. I love you, because _____." When the letter is finished, you can save it for future reference. You can place it in a scrapbook or you can choose to symbolically give the love letter to your loved one. This can be done by burning it and casting the ashes onto the gravesite, burying the letter under a tree or having a helium balloon carry it away in the sky.

- **Write a memorial advertisement:** Place a memorial advertisement in the obituary section of your local paper on your wife's birthday or anniversary. You may want to include her photo and a statement giving your wife credit for something that you learned about life by having been married to her. When the ad comes out, read it and the others that came out on the same day and think about all the love that other families have for their lost loved ones. Clip your ad and save it in your scrapbook. Take joy in the fact that you sent a message of love in the public domain because you want others to know what your wife meant to you.

If you did not experience sharing love letters or notes with each other, do not feel you can't start now or that this task will be a wasted effort. Many people express love in a variety of ways other than writing such as teasing, practical jokes or whatever the case may have been. This exercise, then, is an opportunity for you to express your love in a new way. Embrace it and see what this new experience can do for your grieving and for future benefits with existing relationships.

***

"I wrote e-mails that would make you bawl your eyes out. Writing was a great way to let go of all of the heaviness of the emotions that I was carrying around." –Scott

***

The power of the written word can be life changing. The simple act of writing your thoughts for the other to more fully understand what resounds in your heart is truly a precious gift to give someone you love. I believe the written word can be a method of communication that transcends the real world and approaches that of a spiritual covenant. If we believe that our departed has crossed over to another existence and that their presence is with us, then we know they will truly appreciate this task.

Instructions:

1. Try the love letter or memorial ad as described. Don't fret about writing the greatest love letter or memorial ever written. Writing from your heart is all you need to do, and you will easily reconnect with the spirit of your wife by creating a personal tribute to her memory.

Journaling follow-up:

1. What can I possibly hope to learn from writing a love letter now—after my wife has passed on?
2. How have these efforts to express my feelings via written word helped bring my spirit alive, in a different way than the times when I tried verbal communication?
3. Having placed my feelings down in written form, what have I learned from this experience and what did I do to preserve the privacy of these feelings that I felt for my wife?

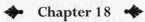 **Chapter 18**

Join the
Chain Gang

Ever get one of those chain e-mails that seem to be forwarded to you from about fifty previous people? Usually they are a joke, a funny picture or an inspirational thought for the day. It is pretty harmless stuff really. It's not too deep philosophically and doesn't really get us thinking about what really matters in life.

However, as a person who is grieving, you are in a unique position to ask people questions that normally would go un-asked. People will share very personal thoughts with you because they want to support you in your grief. The opportunity to ask people to reflect on your loss and relate it to their own lives is rare. Don't let this moment slip away. Rather, seize this precious opportunity for you and others to learn about life's many blessings through the simple act of meaningful communication.

Technology is our friend

The Internet is, of course, a vast resource where widowers can reach out and be supported through their grief. Some great resources are listed in the Resources section at the end of the book, and you are encouraged to check them out. Men are more likely to utilize computer-based resources than women as men are geared to share their feelings in private, whereas women seek out social situations to express their feelings of grief. The

Internet allows men to maintain a sense of privacy, yet gain helpful support with little perceived risk to them. The efficiency of using e-mail with multiple names in the distribution list also eliminates the repetition of making personal one-on-one updates to family and friends when you just don't have the energy or emotional strength to do so. As we see below, Mark's use of e-mails to family and friends provided a much needed sense of reconnection with those who are important in his life, while also preserving his energy and personal grieving process.

***

"We use e-mail as a means to keep in touch with family and friends who live out of state and can't be there for us. Particularly, my deceased wife's aunts and uncles in Florida and friends in Phoenix seem to always drop us a note on special dates like birthdays and anniversaries. They ask all the time how we are doing particularly around those tough times of the calendar." –Mark

***

I used the e-mail resource a few weeks after Terri's death and I found it to be very rewarding. Following Terri's death, I was feeling quite un-inspired, as if there was little, if any, of God's presence in my life. My faith knew better, but no matter how much I tried to convince myself I just didn't feel connected anymore. I didn't get the answer to my prayers, and now my soul mate had left me behind to finish the tasks that I had thought we were going to accomplish together. Raising my sons, seeing them off to college and their weddings, were just a few of the things left undone. I needed to reconnect. So, I e-mailed this question to everyone on my contacts list and waited for replies. I asked, "What inspires you?" I also provided a definition of inspiration that included the phrase of "being in divine spirit" to help insure I would get an answer connected to their beliefs regarding God's presence in their lives.

The response was overwhelming. I read about personal tragedies I previously hadn't heard of from some of my closest friends. They explained how those experiences made them stronger and how they feel that any adversity can now be thrown their way and they would accept it.

I learned that apparent superficial successes were really momentous occasions for celebrating because of the trials it took them to get to their endpoints. Many cited that they could see God's blessings by simply looking at their children. Even though I knew that these stories existed for everyone and I, too, could see God's hand in my sons, reading other widowers' words made it so much more real to me. It helped me to accept the new life before me and to move forward. I believe the conclusions I extracted from this exercise ignited my inspiration to write this book.

Your chain e-mail can be done in a variety of different ways. Here are a couple of ideas to consider.

- Develop an e-mail letter that is distributed to all of your friends asking a philosophical question such as, *What inspires you? What gives you the feeling of being in a divine sense of spirituality?* Ask your friends to reply just to you or to "reply to all". Mention in the body of your letter that "replying to all" is their choice and you will not forward their information to others. But don't be surprised if they do "reply to all", as I found most people are willing to share their thoughts on such topics.
- Ask friends to think of a particular funny event that they shared with your wife and to share that story with you.
- Ask them what they miss the most about your wife. A follow-up question might be to ask them what they appreciate most about *their* spouses.
- Ask them what special trait they think of when they think of your wife.

The neat thing about this activity is the ease in which it can be done and the magnitude of the effect it can have on you and the receivers of your message. The power of communicating on a deep and personal level in important relationships should never be underestimated while we work to overcome obstacles. Try this and see the results for yourself.

Instructions:

1. Pick an idea mentioned or create a question on your own. Develop the question directly about your wife or to a question regarding relationships in general.
2. Collect answers and read them as they come in. You will be surprised that even on questions that were written for relationships in general that your friends will include details describing your wife's impact on their lives.
3. Keep a copy of those e-mails for the scrapbook (chapter 13) or memory box (chapter 12) for future reflection.

Journaling follow-up:

1. How willing have I been to ask others to reflect on their life experiences or a memory/special trait about my wife?
2. What have I learned about myself with this experience, as a means of promoting communication as a deeper and more personal level in relationships?
3. How has this activity helped me learn more about my wife's impact in other lives, specifically in the way others share their personal thoughts with me?

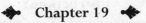

Chapter 19

Go
Natural

I encourage you to get on the Internet or go to your public library and find some examples of photographer Ansel Adams's work. Maybe after you see some of his photographs, you may think to yourself, *Oh yeah, I know this guy! He takes the black and white pictures of our national parks.* Adams's trademark of great pictures like Yosemite Valley is that they are all done in black and white, yet the beauty they capture is astounding. He had no need for color photographs. Adams had the ability to see a panoramic view very differently from the vast majority of us. He saw pure beauty in the graduations of light made unique by the time of day and all the textures and shapes of the land. He was then able to compose the vantage point and capture it all on film to be shared with others. In some respects, his photos are so captivating that color would be a distraction and we would never see the deeper beauty that he is able to show us. To look at one of his photographs is to see so much more than what a personal view of the same site might give.

Why can one person see so much in a scene of nature that we seem too blind to fully appreciate? Soon after the death of a spouse, it is easy to fail to appreciate our natural environment because our emotional connection with it is diluted. Our spouses are not there to share in the appreciation of its beauty and communicate their feelings with us. We now fail to notice a hawk circling high above a farm field, we do not attempt to distinguish between the multitude of colors of a setting sun as we used to do and even when we try to purposefully absorb beautiful vistas, they now seem lackluster and empty. However, we can erase that sense of emptiness by shifting our focus from the sense of loss and the lack of ability to share it with someone to thinking more about what is behind it. If we take the time to look past first glances and appreciate the inner beauty in nature and people, we will become more connected with one another, the divine spirit and therefore our spouses.

Withdrawal during grief desensitizes us to the physical environment as well as disrupts our emotional relationships with others. Other activities in this book focus on strengthening your relationships with others. This activity is focused on jump-starting your recognition of the beauty of the natural world surrounding you, so that you can become reconnected with it and the greater force of which we all are a part.

***

I Need Some Fresh Air

Men have historically been known to have a close connection with the outdoors, whether it is through physical activities, hobbies or occupational and household responsibilities. When surrounded by nature, men demonstrate an improved ability to shift their inward preoccupation with grief outward to appreciating the beauty of nature. The serenity of being in nature tends to infiltrate their inner beings and results in a cleansing of depressing thoughts—even if just for a few hours of the day.

Men from Tom's grief counseling group reported on a variety of activities that reconnected them to nature through which they felt better about themselves and their futures. They mentioned appreciating nature by sitting under a tree, at a beach, by the lake, in one's garden, on a mountain, in a park or even at a dining room table with a single flower in a vase. Several men in the group cited clear benefits from going for a walk. The physical act of putting one foot in front of the other and moving forward was very healing. These connections with nature helped these men reconnect with themselves and with the memories of their lives with their spouses.

Let nature be a way in which you cleanse your mind from the darkness of grief. There are many ways in which you can connect with the outdoors. Sometimes what one needs in a moment of despair is a natural remedy.

***

I gained a strong sense of being reconnected when I was driving home from a long day of traveling all the while thinking of a very important project. On my drive, I was preoccupied with thoughts of how to get the project, which seemed to be stuck, more organized. I was contemplating what my next set of steps needed to be to help me through this stumbling block. Looking at the gas gauge, I saw I was almost on empty so I stopped at a station and soon found myself pumping gas on this late fall afternoon in the countryside of northeastern Wisconsin. While waiting for the pump to stop, I was distracted by an incessant honking. It wasn't the honking of a car horn, but rather the music of over eighty Canadian geese taking off from a nearby cornfield on their southbound migration.

What made the scene even more beautiful was that their quickly developing "V" formation was backlit by a brilliant orange setting sun illuminating the golden cornstalks beneath them. The freshness of a fall afternoon breeze was the final signature of God completing this scene for me to embrace. I was truly struck by the entire image, appreciating the beauty of nature as He had intended it. I felt it was a personalized show despite other people busily running about the station completing their errands. This scene of geese made it perfectly clear to me what needed to get done to solve the organization issue facing my project. I realize the answer was to trust that it will all work out and naturally not force the issue.

Here are some ideas that you might want to consider in order to become reconnected to nature and feel more integrated in it. There are examples on how to do this even if you may not be an outdoors type of person. Be creative in your approach.

- Take a trip to a favorite site that you shared with your wife. Before you go, you might want to remember to bring along some object reminiscent of your wife to leave behind to commemorate the time you spent there. Ask yourself why this place gave you joy and a sense of being connected to each other.

- Scan some images of places shared with your wife and put them on your PC as a slide show screen saver. During the day, you will be reminded of those places that now have an even more special meaning than before.

- Take a trip during the holidays to escape from the excitement that other people may be generating and refocus your thoughts on a meditation away from the maddening crowd. Whether it is a place that you both once shared or a new location, it can provide an opportunity to reflect on nature and your relationship without the added distractions of the holiday. It also provides an escape in which you can take this important time and turn it into a new memory of reflection on your wife. Journal during the trip and record all the locations that stir a different aspect of her memory.

- Add some visual references to nature in your place of work or in your home. Find some inspiring photos taken from a previous trip and have them framed. You can purchase quality prints of famous locations over the Internet and maybe even use a picture as a visual goal to visit there someday.

- Purchase a small indoor water fountain or some houseplants to bring nature inside of your living or work space. You will find it will add an element of peace to this space.

- Locate a birdbath or birdfeeder outside your kitchen window as a great way to attract little creatures of nature you can easily enjoy right outside your home.

***

"Being at our cottage and seeing the beauty of the hostas she planted reminds me of the fun we had and the time we spent with our children and grandchildren. Just being there makes me feel connected to nature and my family—all at the same time. People today are too focused on making money and have lost sight of the other things in life that matter. Take time to smell the roses in life." –Jerry B

***

Make a point to appreciate the beauty of nature today, and look for it where you think you will least find it. No matter how small the example might be, look for it. It may just be noticing a red winged blackbird as you sit waiting at a stoplight and appreciating the wonder of its ability to fly. Think about all that must come together in this world for that bird to be able to be there and have its existence in that moment. Beginning with its birth from an egg to locating an insect today for its lunch, there are infinite connections to a life force to sustain that bird. Ask yourself what continues to drive its heart to beat just one more time.

Think about how your wife came to meet you, marry you and provide you with happiness in the time you spent together. Is this not a miraculous course of events? Of course it is. I believe we are no different than the bird in being sustained in our existence and guided to our destinies with others. Catching these glimpses of nature constantly reminds us that there exists a much larger presence all around us that is in control, every second of the day. Reflecting on examples of nature that are all around us can convince us that this same spiritual life force will carry us into the future. So, stay connected to nature in any way you can.

***

"We didn't have any children so one of the things we did was travel together. I spent a lot of time traveling the world and visiting places that we loved: Germany, Thailand, Las Vegas and Houston. I think in the one-and-a-half years after Kathy died, I flew over 150,000 miles. I just pack and go, particularly when special dates come up on the calendar. By getting away, I don't have to think about things I need to say to people when they ask me how I am doing. It gives me a chance to breathe." –Rick

***

Instructions:

1. Try one or more of the ideas mentioned to reconnect with the natural beauty that surrounds you. Take the time to truly appreciate the detail in specific elements of creation. By noting the details of the world around us, you can find peace in understanding your new place in creation.

Journaling follow-up:

1. What have been one or two situations I have experienced in the past week in which I recognized the beauty of nature?
2. How has my effort to find a greater appreciation of nature affected my degree of pain by the loss of my wife?
3. How has my awareness of the beauty of nature helped me feel connected to the spirit of my wife and of God?

Chapter 20

Light
a Candle

Long ago, the caveman discovered the value of a good fire. It provided a sense of security, kept enemies at bay, provided light, gave warmth and was used to cook food for improvements in diet and health. It even became a means of communication. Today, nothing has really changed in the way that we use fire, with one exception: We use it to symbolize *love*.

We use the flame as a very important symbol in activities of significant meaning to us: baptisms, weddings, church services and so forth. We bring the most basic form of light to these traditions to signal the spirit of love and to remind us of the comfort that love gives us. One candle can cause us to forget the day's stress as we soak in a warm bath. Birthday candles bring smiles to the celebration of another year gone by. The flame's golden glow illuminates only the immediate space around us, casting our faces in warm hues that soften the scene but energize the entire atmosphere. All of these applications signal our love for one another.

By lighting a candle, we activate this sense of energy in all of us. Sometimes the symbol of a candle becomes so powerful, that we catch ourselves gazing into the flame and wind up staring at it, looking for something more inside.

Wives radiate their love to us as a candle radiates its light outward from its source. We often get far too busy or engrossed in what we are doing and simply overlook these rays of love shining upon us. Their love shone and made our lives brighter when they sent a simple teasing note or prepared a bag lunch for us. When we are surrounded by such brightness in light (love), it is easy to overlook until we are in the dark and without it. How did we receive this gift of light from them, and how did we mirror it back? How did we reflect their light onto others? If we think about how we can become extensions of the love around us, we can act upon this to live a more fulfilling life.

***

Light It Up

Men in grief utilize the tradition of lighting a candle less often than women. The rarity with which men use candles does not at all indicate that they are less effective in bringing a sense of tranquility to men. Men simply have not learned as many women have—that candles can be a simple and effective tool for healing.

***

Before Terri's death, my closest connection to candles was at church. As a long time usher, I have the duty to light and then extinguish the candles at the altar to signal the beginning and end of the service. Because of their symbolism of the spirit of God, I consider this task as the most serious part of my duties. When Terri died, the meaning of candles shifted. Whenever she had felt a muscle ache, a cold developing or just wanted time out from a long and busy day, she often took a whirlpool bath and had several lighted candles nearby. Those candles became a symbol of Terri's spirit to me, such that now when I take a whirlpool, I feel compelled to light them in her memory. It is a small but comforting thing to do that adds to my pleasure of the day.

Introducing the spirit of a flame can give you an incredibly satisfying experience that can endure over time. Some ideas to consider are:

- Light a candle and keep it lit all day long in your home. Place it in a prominent location where it will be clearly noticed by you and others throughout the day. Each time it catches your eye, take a moment to look at it and think of a simple way your wife radiated her love to you. You might even take a small candle to your place of work. If you cannot take a candle to work, there are even LED votive lights that mimic a candle. Simpler still, use a small light such as an LED pocket flashlight.

- Organize a candlelight vigil in memory of your wife, the scale of which is totally up to you. A vigil can serve a dual purpose by also calling attention to a problem that you feel needs community action. An example might be if your wife was lost in a car accident caused by a drunk driver or at a poorly designed roadway intersection. You can make this vigil known to local media to help communicate the issue for changing a bad situation for the better so that another person may never experience a loss for the same reason that you did.

- Light a fire in a fireplace, perhaps starting it by burning the regrets letter as described in chapter 32. Keep it burning all day long and think about how your wife's love radiated to you each time you add a log to the fire.

- Hold a bonfire party and, just as in the fireplace, choose to ignite it in a meaningful way. Don't forget the marshmallows to make s'mores for your guests.

***

"The most significant object we have that causes us to reflect on the memory of Mickey is the candle I got from the funeral home. It has her picture on it from a vacation we went on. Its place is typically on the fireplace mantle, but during the holidays, we do something a little different with it. When the family has a gathering for Thanksgiving or Christmas, the candle is always there on the table and we put decorations around it that reflect the holiday." –Mark

***

The symbolism of a flame is a long established concept that brings us back to the importance of love in our lives. Why not include this symbolism in your life to lift your spirit?

Instructions:

1. Try one of the ideas mentioned or think of a way you or your wife had used candles or fire in a meaningful part of your life. Create a new tradition of remembrance each time you go to use a flame in the future.

Journaling follow-up:

1. What is one situation I encountered recently in which I utilized light or flame as a way to symbolize love?

2. When I utilized the symbolism of fire as a reminder of the comfort love gives us, how did this make me feel?

3. In what ways did my wife radiate her love and how did I receive this love? How did I reflect her love-light onto others?

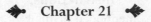
Begin Workouts

Physical activity is God's way of channeling our stress energy into productivity! It is no secret that we feel physically and mentally healthier immediately after a rigorous workout. The pressures from the loss of a wife come from all directions and are of a magnitude unparalleled in any other known circumstance. The effects of stress at this time can be sleeplessness, loss of appetite, irritability and physical pain in our joints and muscles as well as severe headaches. Untreated stress is a primary cause of major illness in the human body, and now is not the time to get sick! There may be other family members depending on you to carry them through the loss, so it's time to shed that stress not only as a preventative measure, but also to lift your mood.

There are two main strategies in counteracting the stress you are experiencing. One is through the use of prescription medications such as antidepressants, sleeping pills and the like, while the other is through more natural means. Physical exertion has been shown to increase levels of messenger chemicals, which allow your body to recondition itself. The brain shifts from sending stress response signaling that results in ailments such as indigestion to endorphin type responses like the feeling of total body relaxation. To reduce and hopefully eliminate the weight that is on your shoulders, try lifting some weights instead!

Please Note: This section is by no means a substitute for your doctor's advice. Sometimes, prescriptions are necessary in order to give yourself some time to adjust. The last thing you need is to add the stress of developing an exercise program on top of more important needs just because your read it here as a *suggestion*. Before starting on any exercise program, consult with your ·doctor to determine what is best for you.

There are a plethora of exercise methods that you can choose from to reduce your stress. Probably the most simple and yet most effective exercise is walking. Walking is the most natural thing humans do besides eating and sleeping. We are designed as bipeds and are therefore meant to walk. Walking also affords us the opportunity to reconnect with our natural surroundings and can allow us the time to talk with a friend. Start off slowly at first and build your stamina gradually. Take this walking time to focus on your breathing. Good breathing techniques can be found in meditation resources. Learn to breathe fully and in a manner of detoxification. Yes, breathing eliminates toxins from your body just as your waste streams and sweating do. Soon you will find walking an activity you don't want to miss.

***

The Pressure Relief
Men have to be willing to become more resourceful once their wives are gone if they wish to heal their grief and move towards positive reflections on their pasts. Reaching out to others for emotional support and improving their own personal health through stress relieving exercise are just two ways that can have significant and positive outcomes. Men need to learn that just as physical exercise can stimulate the body into rebuilding itself into a healthier physical state, sharing emotional thoughts of concern with others also exercises the mind to transform a distressful state into feelings of well-being. In Joe's case, see how he channels his grief into constructive behaviors that release his physical stress through exercise and his emotional release through the friendships he developed.

***

"You have to be active and not sit around the house all day. I definitely don't sit in a bar. Instead, I've joined the YMCA and a Veteran's group shortly after Marge died. I golf at least once a week and I work out routinely and it is a really good way to get your mind off of things and feeling better about yourself. At the Y, I bump into people I know all the time and the talking we do while we work out makes me glad I went— even if we end up talking about politics and how to solve the world's problems." –Joe

***

My personal favorite for exercising is walking. Terri and I often walked the neighborhood streets, which I found to have several benefits. First, it accommodated time to talk with each other. The daily pressures of working, managing a household and raising two sons left limited time for quality interaction. Those walks were invaluable in communication benefits alone! Secondly, our walks afforded opportunities to relieve stress by getting out and connecting to nature. We live near a small lake where wildlife is often seen. On our walks, we oftentimes witnessed Canadian geese or deer foraging for food. Lastly, I always felt better after walking off a great dinner and slept better too. Walking truly became a habit, and I missed it greatly shortly after Terri passed away.

Then I took the time to fit walking into my schedule as a single father. This time however, while the benefits are the same, I now talk with my sons. In order to encourage their participation, we must bring along a football to throw as we walk. These walks take a little more effort now that I need to improve my arm strength, but they are well worth it!

If walking seems a little mundane to you, why not revisit a physical activity that you used to do in your youth? Remember back when physical activity was a natural means to making you happy? Running cross-country, playing football, softball or just a pick-up basketball game on the playground made you smile even during intense physical exertion! Old interests can easily be translated today into playing catch with your child or joining a league. Skiing, bicycling and jogging are very popular sports adults regularly do that can have the same end result, while allowing you to relive something you truly enjoyed in earlier and happier times.

You could also sign up for an exercise class with a friend at the local gymnasium or YMCA. Even if a friend is not readily available, join anyway and you'll meet people in the process. There are a variety of well-known choices like swimming, yoga and acrobics as well as newly created sports like dodgeball. Check in and see how some of these newer sports are taking off in popularity.

Don't forget that one of the key points here is to make this exercise activity an enjoyable time to interact with others and just plain fun. If it feels more like exercise than fun, try shifting to a different activity to bring the enjoyment back into the experience. Why not sign up for that ballroom dance instruction that you and your wife wanted to do so long ago? Not only will you be learning something new and useful, but you will also be having fun, reducing your stress and helping your body stay healthy.

Whatever you choose to do, make your exercise plan enjoyable and engaging or you will soon stop doing it. When your body gets the exertion it needs, sleep will come easier, headaches will diminish and your appetite will stabilize.

Instructions:

1. Think through your past participation in sports and reconnect with those activities. Mix it up to keep yourself interested.
2. Start simple at first and gradually ramp it up to have a routine. Make a commitment to improving your body's health.
3. Get involved with a friend or just do it and meet new friends along the way.
4. Join a class not only to improve your health, but also to learn something new along the way like yoga, dancing or skiing.
5. Stick with it. If you find yourself dropping a plan, try something new.

Journaling follow-up:

1. What specific methods of exercise have I been able to incorporate into my daily life since losing my wife?
2. How has this activity provided me a sense of enjoyment and an opportunity to engage with others?
3. How have I noticed my exercise routine affecting my level of stress related to the loss of my wife?

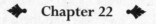
Remember
Your Song

Couples often refer to the song that was playing when they first met as "our song". The song reconnects them to the past and actually provides a visual as well as auditory memory trigger of the moment when they met. We can recall the specific attire worn that evening, the weather and the ambiance of the setting all because our memories are strengthened through a meaningful song. The sound of music has the power to bring many different thoughts and emotions to mind. We use this powerful invention of man to celebrate, worship, relax, have fun and to comfort us. Music is so powerful when used or connected to an event, that sometimes when it is heard long after the event has transpired, we immediately think of the event and re-enter the frame of mind we experienced long ago. In a way, it helps us do a better job of recalling our pasts; it is a time travel enhancement for our memories.

***

"My wife Gloria loved music and was an excellent dancer. It was too bad she married a guy with two left feet!" –Jerry B.

***

Music can be a trigger for both happy and sad emotional release. Just driving in the car with the feeling of low energy after a long day of work can be quickly turned around by hearing an energizing favorite song on the radio. For me, nothing beats a good hard rock and roll song from the late 1970s to get me back on track! Yet, there are those songs that also trigger emotional releases of sadness. I always am reminded of a tragic time when I hear the Nazareth song "Love Hurts". This song was being played over and over on the radio at a time when a friend of mine was killed in a skiing accident during a high school ski trip. To this day, I am reminded of Scott's tragic accident whenever the song is played.

***

It's All About the Music

Men and women in grief experience a similar yearning to hang onto past memories of their loved ones to preserve a sense of present connectedness with them. Music makes this reconnection process much easier for the bereaved to do. Though the recollection of certain songs will trigger a roller coaster of both happy and sad emotions, men will ultimately experience powerful senses of comfort as they feel their loved ones continuing to be guiding spirits in their life journeys.

***

There are a few songs that trigger my sadness when I think about the difficulties Terri and I endured trying to combat her cancer. Some days when I hear these songs on the radio I let them play in honor of her memory. Oftentimes, I actually feel she causes me to turn on the radio at the very instant a song is playing so that I will be reminded of her, as a form of her communicating something of importance to me or to just let me know she is with me. However, there are days when I need to turn the music off, because I just can't bear that specific memory while something else that is sad is going on in my life.

This radio communiqué happened one day as I was driving back home from a visit with my father. I needed to attend a funeral to offer my comfort to a dear friend of Terri's. Terri's friend had lost her daughter who, like Terri, was in the prime of her life. As I was nearing home, I wondered what possible words I could ever tell her that would be comforting, knowing that her daughter left young children behind, amongst other tragic aspects of her passing. As this question revolved in my mind,

I turned on the radio and heard the one song that always reminds me of the time we were informed that Terri's cancer was terminal. This song's message to me is that we are not immortal. Hearing it that day sent a very strong feeling through me that my message to her friend should be that Terri still was with me and with her in her moment of need and that her daughter was now in God's arms. There is no question that I feel Terri's presence routinely and that the songs I hear are just one way I am reassured of that.

You might already have felt similar experiences. If you have, treat them as messages that your wife is still with you, confirming that your thoughts are indeed on the right track. Whenever a trigger reminds us of our loved ones, whether it brings joy or sadness, consider these memories as good ones because these feelings acknowledge the profound effect your wife had on your life. Take these feelings as a sign of comforting knowledge that this connection continues spiritually. If you have not experienced such a connection, then this activity will enhance your ability to catch these moments in your day.

You should find this activity to be a lot of fun as well as an uplifting experience for your spirit. There were so many different ways that music touched your lives, so create for yourself a lasting audio memorial by tapping into these activities. Here are a few ideas to consider:

- Take a moment to generate a list of songs that are meaningful for the two of you. Do not just include the romantic songs you shared. Add in songs that represent the fun times as well. Compile a song list that reminds you of your wife and the times you shared together. The list could include:

  a. "Your song"

  b. Music your wife played on an instrument

  c. Songs from your dating days

  d. Songs played at your loved one's celebration of life or funeral service (this may need to be on a separate disk as these will conjure up feelings of sadness as compared to the others on the list).

- Collect the songs, group them by genre and burn them onto CDs or your MP3 list for when you want to reconnect with them. If you do not have CD burning skills to create your favorite songs list, ask around because many of your friends or younger people are quite adept at doing this. With today's software, you can even make a CD label with your wife's picture on it to personalize it even more. You could even play the mix at a memorial party you hold in her memory.
- Make a focused effort to learn to appreciate her favorite music even if it is different from your own interests. Read a book about her favorite musician or musical genre if one has been written. You may gain a little more appreciation for why she liked her favorite music and some insight into her personal values.
- Move your wife's favorite CDs to your vehicle or add them to your MP3 player. Listen to her music for an instant connection to her soul.
- Memorize the lyrics to her favorite song. You may want to add a music section and a copy of these lyrics to the scrapbook activity of chapter 13, "Gather a Scrapbook."
- Invite a friend to attend a concert that your wife would have enjoyed. Reflect on the music as a symbol of your wife's spirit and discuss with your friend how the music made you feel and why your friend believes your wife would have enjoyed it.
- Call a radio station and ask the disc jockey to play a favorite song that reminds you of your wife as a tribute to her memory. You may want to do this on her birthday, anniversary or another day of significance to you.

These are just a few ideas to keep the memory of your wife alive in simple formats to which you will have ready access. You can play this music in your home, car and office as instant connections to her essence.

Instructions:

1. Try one or all of the ideas listed above, or think of something that may even be more directly attributed to your wife's love of music. You will find that by doing so, you will have created a lasting memorial of your relationship because of the longevity that music plays in your everyday life.

Journaling follow-up:

1. What specific activity have I done recently to use music as a method of connecting with my wife's memories?
2. What emotions have I experienced when I hear specific music that triggers memories of my wife?
3. Why do I think these experiences of hearing certain songs help to reinforce my belief in my wife's continued presence in my life?

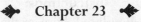

Chapter 23

Frame
Memories

The love between you and your wife took many forms. Perhaps you demonstrated this love quite plainly for others to witness. You held hands during a walk, kissed each other while dancing and gave each other hugs as one of you left for travel. Love for one's spouse can be displayed in so many ways, it seems infinite. In fact, the act of having a child and raising him or her as committed parents demonstrates the love that was shared ever so strongly.

This activity will put a small sample of the love once shared between you and your wife on display; there is no reason why you can't continue to illustrate your love for your wife now. The point is not to build a shrine to your wife in every room of your home and remain focused on the past. The idea is to celebrate her life and what it meant to you. This celebration can be tasteful, long lasting and respectful no matter what new relationships life brings you. This activity acknowledges the time that you spent with your wife, a part of your life that should not be hidden from view.

***

Dropping Anchor
Men in grief often rely on the use of photos as "anchors" to retain memories of happier times in their lives while their spouses were alive.

Many have strong needs to hang onto the emotional bond with these photos as they represent direct connections to their pasts. Men and women alike are fearful that they will fall short in their abilities to recall past events due to the potential infirmities of aging, and some see the use of photos as their "security blanket" in maintaining the connection with their deceased spouses. However, men typically have been found to be less particular and dedicated to the use of "framed memories" than women, as women are more attune to taking photos and organizing them in this detailed fashion. Once again, men can benefit from doing the activities in this chapter.

***

When I perused the keepsakes Terri had given to me long before her illness, I experienced the power of this task almost instantaneously. Many years ago, Terri made a needlepoint card for our wedding anniversary and gave it to me. There was a simple but incredibly powerful phrase framed in a heart on the paper card that reads, "Love Is All There Is." Truer words regarding our relationship could never exist, as love is truly what we shared. In the end, love was all there was as cancer slowly erased her physical existence, but I feel that Terri's love endures. She had given me that needlepoint heart many years prior to falling ill, but it meant so much to me that I had kept it in my dresser drawer all those years. After Terri's death, I looked for something to signify what she meant to me. I wanted something prominently displayed in my home. When I came upon this card, it was a very easy decision to choose it as a tribute to our love for one another. I completed the framing project with one special touch. I photocopied her message to me from the inside of the card and affixed it to the backside of the frame. Someday, when that frame is taken down to be moved or given away, the rest of the story will be seen again as written on the back.

This is an easy project to accomplish and it is one of the most rewarding to complete. Not only will you be preserving an artifact of her life in a meaningful way, but you will also have the enjoyment of sharing it with those who visit your home. Remember the intent here is not to adorn each room with framed memories, but to do this in a manner that focuses on that one key tribute. Therefore, choose your framed remembrance item with care so that her true spirit and your relationship are reflected.

***

"I put a number of photos together as a collage and when I retire for bed, I give one picture a tap as I walk by and make a comment. That is my connection to great memories." –Jerry B.

***

Find a special item that has significance to you that captures the spirit of your wife, the love you each shared or both! It would be an especially good choice if it was created by your wife and hopefully had some written words from your loved one. However, don't fret if you can't find such an item. Here are some other examples that can be equally special:

- **Artwork:** Any artwork, sketches, engineering drawings, sewing or even doodles from a piece of scrap paper can easily be framed into an artistic tribute to your wife. Don't be afraid to use more than one sketch or detail drawing in the same frame. It might even take the form of a collage.
- **A shadow box:** Military or sports awards, even the badge emblem pried off from her favorite car that she loved to drive coupled with photos can be a creative and telling story about her life.
- **A dried flower:** Preserve a flower from your wife's funeral or life celebration service. This can be either pressed or dried and placed under a glass dome or framed.
- **A portrait:** Have a talented artist paint a portrait from your favorite photo. In this medium, the mood of the portrait can be adjusted by changing the clothing or background. Ask the artist for ideas on how to capture your wife's true spirit.

A good choice is something that is suitable for framing or easily displayed as a tribute of your love. If you frame the object, I encourage you to add a special message to be affixed to the rear of the frame to help capture the spirit of the memorial. Include information such as when the object was crafted, on what occasion it was given, etc. When people ask about the framed item, you can choose to show them the back of the frame or not, but know that it is there for all to see as a remembrance of your relationship.

***

"I spend a lot of time on my laptop computer. So one of the things I did was place pictures of her on my background of the PC." –Rick

***

Women, Children & Photos First

It is common practice for families to hang pictures of family members throughout their houses, regardless of the fact that these family members are often still present and a vital part of each other's lives. This practice reinforces the emotional need to utilize photos as a visual reminder of the memories that one hangs onto as one strives to maintain a connection to past and present memories. We see the examples of Jerry B. (framed photo) and Rick (computer background) as illustrations of this point.

The importance photos play in healing grief can be explained in another way: Consider how family members often identify a photo album as the one personal item they would toss out the window in the event of a fire. This instinctive reaction reiterates the high value photos play as a direct connection to loved ones. The fear of losing this connection to the happier times of the past can create an overwhelming sense of grief. Don't needlessly add to your stress. Organizing cherished photos in a display is a great memorial and means to anchor one's memories to happier times.

***

Instructions:

1. Use one of the ideas mentioned as a guide, or create one of your own framed memorials. If you can't think of an idea, ask a friend or family member to help you with this task. Remember that your local craft or framing store can be a great resource to help you.

Journaling follow-up:

1. What is one special item that captures the love we each shared, and how will I choose to display this item?
2. How do I feel about sharing this item with those who visit our home?
3. Why does this item capture my wife's true spirit and the meaning of our relationship?

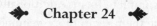
Send a Message

W hen suffering the loss of loved ones, it is only natural to desire one last chance to communicate with them. Soon after these loved ones are gone, many survivors have frequent thoughts about the lost opportunity to communicate with their deceased spouses on important topics. If only we had just one more chance to talk with them, then maybe we could let go and feel more complete! However, in reality, we would never be able to satisfy our internal needs no matter how much more time we had. This activity is designed to collect our thoughts more completely so as to help fulfill that need for one last shared conversation.

There is something special about writing down our thoughts on paper. Speech is fluid, while text is not. Speech is typically interactive as we continuously change our line of thought as we react to listeners. Hence, the conversation evolves and can easily be diverted from the main ideas that you may want to share in a more direct and meaningful manner. By writing your thoughts down, you are able to focus on them exclusively, therefore eliminating the risk of being distracted and omitting important issues. The written word also makes our message more meaningful, because we have taken the time to write it down.

Writing helps us to organize our thoughts so that they are not rambling and disjointed. It allows the content to more perfectly express our thoughts in their complete form. Additionally, if we write our inner most feelings, we make them seem more genuine to the reader, because written documentation carries with it a sense of permanence. There are many ways to transmit these written thoughts: mail them, send them electronically or put them down in a journal. Whatever method you choose to convey your thoughts, the message will be even more special if you take the time and effort to insure the message's permanence.

***

Learning to Journal

Journaling can help the writer sort out emotions, increase focus, build self-esteem, manage stress, problem solve, relinquish the past and resolve conflicts with others. Experts believe that investigating such areas through writing builds understanding of oneself and allows one to become better at making decisions that are in line with one's values and goals.

In addition to these emotional benefits, research has shown that journaling can improve physical health. Expressive writing can improve blood pressure, depression, asthma, arthritis, cognitive functioning and strengthen the immune system. People who engage in expressive writing report feeling happier and less negative soon after writing. Similarly, reports of depressive symptoms, rumination and general anxiety tend to drop in the weeks and months after writing about emotional upheavals.

When people compose their complex emotions into a story and approach their issues from different perspectives, they gain the maximum benefit of the journaling experience. The act of constructing a story allows people to make better sense of events and memories that they may not have earlier understood. In many cases, the writer is surprised to learn that the real issues are different from the ones that they had anticipated.

Like every therapeutic technique, expressive writing may not suit everyone. Certain personality types tend to respond better to writing than others, and writing's effectiveness may be compromised by how the individual handles stress, the ability to self-regulate and the quality of interpersonal relationships. But for many, expressive writing can be intensely therapeutic and for a few, literally life-changing.

***

I have written many times to Terri and some examples are sprinkled throughout this book. The power of writing was very evident and effective in our relationship. We used to put Post-It notes to each other in the most unlikely spots where they might have remained for days prior to their discoveries. Then there were the simple notes of a request to start dinner or perform an errand for the other, but always signed with a simple "Love". Now that she is gone and there is no point to leaving notes hidden about the house, I find solace in journaling my thoughts for the day. Even though I might only write a paragraph because I am so tired, I feel she hears these thoughts. For some reason, writing the words is much more meaningful to me than simply thinking about them. If there was one thing that I learned to do to keep our relationship strong, it was to communicate, and I always had success in writing my thoughts down for her so that she could see and understand my perspective. I take great comfort in knowing that she read these thoughts then and continues to do so with every thought I write today.

Unlike the letters described in chapter 17 or chapter 32, this activity is meant to plainly focus on capturing your thoughts. Once done, you may or may not want to think more on the subject. Once you begin the practice of writing for clarifying your perspectives and mindset on a variety of issues and experiences, you will begin to find a greater sense of resolution to your sense of being.

To get started, you may want to purchase a journal and place it in a convenient location that is readily accessible. Find the best time of the day when you will not be disturbed so that you can really focus on your most important concerns. It also helps to get in a comfortable position so that you can more easily get into the flow of writing should you want to write for a longer period. You don't want to be interrupted several times to adjust your chair, the lighting or any other environmental distraction when you want to dig deep into your consciousness and have an effective writing session.

Some other specific ideas to try to include:

- Write a detailed history of your lives together that covers all of the topics you can think of such as:
  a. The time you first met
  b. Getting married
  c. Having your children
  d. Time of trials you both endured
  e. Moving and sharing in each other's successes
  f. Your feelings of loss (regret, anger, sadness, commitment, etc.)
- Write a poem or other personal letter on the event of an anniversary date of some sort, birthday or other significant date in your life. You may want to do this annually and keep the entries in your journal for posterity.
- Write a short story about one event in your life with your wife. It could be a funny experience on a vacation or how you first met— any chapter in your life will do. Use a specific story that you find to be particularly interesting and meaningful to describing what happiness your wife gave you.
- Write your own personal memoirs. This would make an excellent gift to younger family members long after you pass away.
- Think of a way to "transmit" the letter. Ideas include:
  a. Place in a bottle, seal it and cast it into a favorite body of water.
  b. Place it inside an envelope and have a helium balloon carry it away.
  c. Bury it near your wife's final resting spot or at a favorite location where you both shared in a cherished experience.

***

"When the day of her birthday came four months after she died, I did not even feel like celebrating it in any way. Her birthday just served as a reminder of what the boys and I no longer had with us. But I knew it was important for my sons to celebrate their mother that day. So we got some helium balloons. Then I had the boys each write a note to their mom and

I did as well. We tied the notes to the balloons and released them from the back deck of the house. It seemed like a fitting thing to do." –Scott

***

Do not underestimate the therapeutic power that writing can bring to you. Spending time alone with just some paper and a pen is one of the few ways that you can get in touch with your innermost thoughts and feelings. Keep in mind that whatever you write is plenty good enough because after all, it is only for your benefit and not necessarily for others to critique. Give it a try, and even a small start may turn into something that can benefit others as well as yourself. After all, this is how this book got started!

Instructions:

1. Try the journaling technique even if you think that writing isn't for you. Even the simplest thoughts written on paper will have a large effect on improving your understanding of the relationship you had with your wife. It might even become a lifelong habit!
2. Try one of the ideas mentioned in this chapter or create a unique writing exercise of your own.

Journaling follow-up:

1. What is a method of creating a message that makes me feel most comfortable?
2. In what ways have I found writing about my life experiences and perspectives helpful in getting in touch with my innermost thoughts and feelings?
3. How has my practice of writing helped fulfill my need for conversation with my wife?

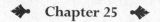

Chapter 25

Create a
Comforting Object

Why are men so emotionally clueless? Blame the male brain. "Men are hard-wired differently," says David Powell, Ph.D., president of the International Center for Health Concerns, who explains that the connection between the left brain (a home of logic) and the right (the seat of emotions) is much greater in women. "Women have the equivalent of an interstate highway, so they move readily between the right and left brains. For men the connection is like a meandering county lane, so we don't have such ready access to feelings."

Males are conditioned from an early age not to tune in to emotions. Boys learn at an early age the lesson of eat fast, talk loud, compete ferociously and keep your feelings under guard. Showing emotions is a no-can-do among men. By age one, they make less eye contact than girls and pay more attention to moving objects like cars than to human faces. Both mothers and fathers talk less about feelings (except anger) to sons than daughters and boys' vocabularies include fewer feeling words. In the playground, boys learn to choke back tears and to show no fear. Their faces, once as openly emotional as those of girls, become less expressive as they move through the elementary school years. Boys, as they grow up to be men, feel continual societal pressures and personal expectations to maintain their masculine persona in living out the message of big boys don't cry.

Men use fewer words, and when they talk in public they put themselves in a one-up situation—unlike women, who talk to draw others closer. Even with friends, men mainly swap information as they talk shop, sports, cars or computers. However, as gender roles and rules have loosened, some men have dared to let their softer sides show. Creating a teddy bear or an alternative symbol provides a much needed sense of both physical and emotional comfort, as men look for the opportunity to return to their childhoods, when they may have been allowed a greater degree of innocence and acceptance of their non-masculine feelings.

***

Do you remember a favorite toy that provided you comfort when you were a young child, such as a blanket, stuffed teddy bear or other consoling plaything? You probably gave the object a name and dragged it everywhere you went. Probably it was particularly important to you when you were in bed sick or when you were sad, because it gave you a special sense of comfort. Eventually, it became tattered from the frequent use and from countless trips through the washing machine. It was probably patched many times over, a button replacing a missing eye or similar mends to give the object new life, because your mother knew how much you treasured that little stuffed piece of security.

Inevitably, these comforting toys wear out and fall to the wayside as we begin to count more on our relationships with others to get us through the tough times. These personal relationships can be so significant that we count on them routinely and sometimes take for granted the uplifting feelings that they give us, which help us to survive our lowest points. Then we discover that these treasured relationships are like the stuffed bear: They do not last forever.

I decided to have a teddy bear crafted from a favorite piece of Terri's clothing. The choice to use Terri's bathrobe was an easy one. She loved wearing it and it gave her much comfort. Her weaknesses for her robe and flannel pajamas were well known by everyone in the family. Living in northern Wisconsin, you learn to appreciate added warmth on January nights!

Fortunately, the robe had enough material to make three bears: one for each son and one for me. We were so pleased upon receiving them that I asked the maker if it was possible to also make pajamas for the bears from Terri's favorite PJs. Since then, my bear has sat on a chair in my bedroom and it bestows upon me a comforting presence that I cannot adequately describe. There are days, long days, when I am about to turn in for the night, that I look at that bear and feel empowered—that I am fulfilling my promise to be the best provider and parent to my sons. Other times, I gaze upon the bear and feel that I receive a different look of playfulness when something has particularly poked fun at me earlier in the day.

That bear grants me a different type of a connection, a truly unique conduit, to share my thoughts in a playful yet comforting manner that I cannot experience through any other method or means. Unlike your favorite childhood toy, the loss of your wife was reciprocal; she gave you seemingly infinite support in return for the support you gave her during your relationship. This loss is not as ethereal, it is substantive and as real as it can get. As an adult, you know the true basis of a supportive spousal relationship and can now reflect on the substance of the many memories you shared with her.

***

"Marnie had kept her baby blanket since she was born. So, it was very clear that it was an object of real value to her and now it was for us to decide what to do with it. After some thought, we cut the blanket up and some went to her dad and brother, some were placed in the coffin and the last pieces went into some picture frames for the boys. Within that framed piece of blanket was a picture of their mother. It was a great way to share one of her possessions with the people whom she loved."–Ross

***

As we've noted earlier, the death of a spouse has been described as the most difficult stress a person will ever experience. In spite of the support provided by family and friends, sometimes we just need a symbol of comfort to assure us that everything is okay. But where we once reached for a teddy bear or security blanket for reassurance, we can utilize the idea of using a spiritual symbol. This activity creates a memento crafted directly from the clothing of your wife. It brings her spirit into a new creation to be with you in your moments of need.

Instructions:

1. Find a favorite piece of clothing that your wife cherished or always wore. It can be a bathrobe, a flannel shirt, maybe even a particular blanket or comforter she used by the fireplace on winter nights. Choose something that clearly was specifically hers and something she used regularly.

2. Decide on what new creation will give you the most satisfaction and usefulness in its new form. Suggestions include: a teddy bear or other stuffed animal, a throw pillow, a quilt or other small blanket.

3. Find a person capable of constructing this new comfort toy from the article(s) of clothing you have. Use your network of friends, co-workers or friends of your wife to find this person. Ask around, you will be surprised at how many talented people are within your direct network of friends. Also, many talented seamstresses can be found in women's church groups, craft shops or even in the phone book as seamstresses or tailors.

4. Discuss with the person you choose what you would like to have made. The person is usually resourceful enough to know either where to purchase a pattern or even how to make up a pattern before the clothing is even cut. Discuss the cost and don't be surprised if the person does it at little or no cost to you, particularly if they know you or your wife.

Journaling follow-up:

1. What favorite piece of clothing did my wife frequently wear, and how can it be transformed into a new and comforting piece?

2. How has this activity helped me face the reality that relationships do not last forever?

3. How has this new memento helped to become a new symbol of love and comfort so that my wife's spirit continues to live within me?

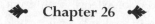

Chapter 26

Celebrate

Some people beyond your immediate household may feel a sense of loss when your wife passes away. Family, friends and co-workers also share needs to pay their respects and say final goodbyes because of their connection to your wife during her life. There are many traditions from very small and discrete ones to grand celebrations that can last for days. For example, the Deep South is famous for funeral processions with upbeat songs such as "When the Saints Go Marching In." Some people hold wakes where people gather and share a meal, bringing together those whose lives were touched by your deceased wife. There are various means to share comfort and reflect on memories of your wife.

However, within a few months to a year, particularly on your wife's birthday or on your wedding anniversary, you may feel alone in missing your wife's presence. Because friends have not been calling lately, it is easy to think they have forgotten the importance of the approaching date. Perhaps the friends who normally would have been involved in celebrating your wife's birthday feel hesitant to mention the date as it approaches. They are unsure as to how you may want to acknowledge the significance of the event. In the end, the decision comes down to minimizing the date or acknowledging it by turning it into another chance to celebrate the life of your lost loved one.

A satisfying way to acknowledge such events is to plan a memorial party. Yes, a party! The funeral and services held back when your wife's death was fresh in your heart carried a lot of sorrow. The sadness deepened as you later thought about all the future opportunities that would never be realized. However, now that some time has passed, take this opportunity to memorialize the person in a fun way, reflecting primarily on the happier times you both shared. Your focus can shift to all of the good that you received from having known your wife. This is especially a positive event when the person had a spirit of fun and compassion for others.

***

Let Me Be!

You may wonder how you can be expected to celebrate at any time after losing the love of your life. It is not suggested that you push yourself through the various phases, emotions or therapies associated with grief! As stressed several times in this book already, grief is an individual process and only you can do the work towards repairing your life in a manner that fits you. Performing tasks that do not feel comfortable to you is not building for a better tomorrow, but reflecting on the concept behind them will give you insight into how you are feeling at this point in the grieving process.

The eventual transition through grief into aspects of celebrating and recalling fond memories of your loved one is most often a similar process for men and women alike. Creating moments to celebrate, whether by yourself or with family and friends, provides an opportunity for you and others to reflect on the positive influences your spouse had on those she touched. These moments of celebrating will also help you retain memories that will help promote the transition from grief to one of gratitude for the life you shared together.

***

Terri and I attended many dinners, holiday parties and other entertainment events that were hosted by our friends. In fact, over the years we enjoyed them so much that some of these events became traditions. After Terri's death, I was inclined to decline the ongoing invitations I received, but I made it a point to continue my involvement in spite of attending without a companion. I found that continuing gave me a way to show Terri's circle of friends that they were equally important to me. I took it a step further by trying to host a Halloween party myself, complete with bottled beer and soda imported from around the world, and I even had a professional Tarot card reader in attendance. Our friends brought the snacks and it all came together even though all that I sent out was an e-mail invite a short while in advance. Several times during the party, someone brought up a funny incident that they had experienced with Terri and it really made me feel as if her spirit was there. The party was a hit and in addition to that, everyone compared notes about what their future might hold as foretold by the fortune teller!

***

"We had some of Marnie's closest friends come over and go through hundreds and hundreds of pictures that everybody brought over. The kids really had some fun looking back at Marnie's life and hearing the many stories of her life–from childhood to her last days. The pictures made us all talk about many stories of her life. We literally stayed up the entire night going through her life that was laid out in photos." –Ross

***

Holding a party can be as elaborate or as simple as you choose it to be. Ask a close friend of your wife to help plan the event. Note that it does not have to cost you any money. To reduce or even eliminate the cost to you, host a potluck that divides up the cost and preparation effort among the attendees. Here are some specific ideas to consider:

- A memorial golf outing: A memorial golf outing is easy to plan and a perfect idea particularly if the deceased was into the game. Send out an invite and get a final list of attendees and coordinate the tee times with the golf course. You might even award humorous certificates of performance (cheaply printed from your computer) to laugh at afterward over burgers in the clubhouse.
- A traditional backyard cook out: This can be a B.Y.O.M. (bring your own meat) party with others bringing the condiments, snacks and lawn chairs. You supply the grill and the backyard!

- A dinner party held at a restaurant: If your wife liked to dine out, plan a party at her favorite restaurant. This could be arranged as a holiday party. Toast your loved one's memory and good friends!
- A wine & cheese party: If your wife liked wine, this just might be a unique and creative way to continue celebrating her spirit with others. Share her favorite wine with your friends.
- A football game tailgate party: A perfect fit, especially if your wife was a big fan. Make up some stickers or a button that says the team has a supporter in heaven. Planning several weeks or months in advance may be required due to ticket availability.
- A garden party: Were you and your wife flower enthusiasts? This get-together could even help you get some much-needed work done. Invite attendees to come over to help plant some flowers or rake leaves as the deceased did and you provide the beverages!
- A fundraiser party: How about a bowling for dollars campaign? Here, partygoers pledge a nickel per pin on their score. Break up the group into teams to make it competitive and donate the money raised to your wife's favorite charity.

Any of these outings would be the perfect time to share funny stories about your wife, or to bring up her favorite quotes or lines she used to say at some point in the party or outing. Consider giving a little speech to offer your gratitude for the help these guests provided you during your hardest times of grief. If you feel too emotional to do this, maybe just writing your thank-you note down on a card and placing it on a snack table would suffice as well. This is a great way to say thank you to those who were there for you in your time of need.

The scale and the extent of the planning are up to you. You may find that the event is so much fun that it becomes an annual affair.

Instructions:

1. Do one of the ideas mentioned or create a party of your own as a way to celebrate the life and memory of your wife.

Journaling follow-up:

1. What type of party would provide the best opportunity to focus on the positive and happier times I shared with my wife?

2. How did I feel about hosting a party as a way to "celebrate" my wife's life?

3. What were some stories shared by others and myself of my wife, which reflected on the happy times that we shared?

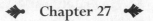

Chapter 27

Plant a
Memorial Garden

When we lose someone very dear to us, we long for something that will provide some lasting sense of connection to them. We fear we will forget the small things the person used to say or do that would make our days more complete. The sense of emptiness pervades our existence. Other activities in this book intend to capture those smaller things that defined who your wife was when she was with you. The next activity helps you create a living reminder that will provide an *ongoing* tribute to your spouse. Memorial gardens or a memorial planting are a good way to create new beauty on the earth with the purposeful slant of remembrance.

Memorial gardens are not new, nor should they be limited to cemeteries, parks or sports facilities named only for the rich and famous. This can be anything from a small flower box outside an urban window to a large garden in a city park. It can simply be one planting of a tree or a potted plant in the house. All will be a natural tribute to your deceased wife. A tree will be especially uplifting as the years go by and long after the house is sold because you will be able to drive by and still see your tribute and be reminded of the woman it commemorates.

***

"We planted an evergreen tree in the memory of Gloria, and it's known as Gloria's tree. The whole family helped in choosing the type of tree and digging the hole and even by adding fertilizer to it. When I look at that tree, it makes me think of her, particularly because she always loved being outside digging in the garden." —Jerry B.

***

A Memorial as Lovely as a Tree

During the course of over twenty years of counseling widowers like Jerry B., Tom has met numerous men who seized the opportunity to create their own memorial garden in various forms. These men and their families found great comfort in doing so because it provided a lasting sense of connection in a coordinated tribute to their loved ones. The most popular type of memorial garden has been the planting of a wife's favorite tree.

***

I had the benefit of having some good friends offer to plant a tree for me in Terri's memory. We decided that to symbolize her never-ending spirit, an evergreen would be a great choice. Every morning, I look out my breakfast window and can see that evergreen growing taller. In many years to come, I know that it will provide shelter to many animals and birds as well as stand tall and green even in the coldness of winter. This living symbol warms my heart especially knowing it was a gift from good friends.

We appreciated the beauty that we saw in our spouses. If one takes the time to look, we can see that sort of natural beauty all around us. A perfect example is the wide spectrum of beauty given to us by flowers. We give flowers to one another to show our love. We use them to brighten the hospital rooms of the ill. For some of us, certain flowers even carry special meanings. Certain trees or plants may remind us of our childhood home. Every time I see the bright red leaves of a maple tree in autumn, I think of the large maples my parents had at the home where I grew up. There are many living plants that are excellent to use to memorialize your wife.

I visit Terri's grave site on significant dates of the year routinely to honor her memory. It takes little effort to make her site decorated to match the seasons of the year. For example, Terri was born in October, so I brought a fall flower arrangement to her site for her birthday. I feel it is a simple way to illustrate that my thoughts are with her on such special days as those.

There are many different variations of this activity. You can plant a tree with a memorial plaque at its base. The marker can be a simple rock with hand painted lettering or a professionally made plaque or stone engraved with her name. If space is at a premium, why not plant a flowerbox and add a few trinkets that represent her interests in life. For example, one could have a small bonsai tree and make a diorama with small figurines for a person who loved camping or fishing.

Sometimes a person's shoes reflect who that person was in life. A pair of high top sneakers or a pair of boots she loved would make a great planter for some flowers on a porch step. The ideas are endless. Just think of something she liked to do and add that element to your garden. Maybe it is something as simple as making the garden into a notable shape such as a heart or including a sundial if she loved stargazing. You might even go as far as to bury a time capsule under the marker that contains a poem or other items as a tribute.

Instructions:

1. Think of a memorial garden that can best suit your situation and scale it up or down to match the space that is available to you. Remember that this can be a flower box, a bonsai plant or a full-scale outdoor garden. Collect some garden accents that can help depict the memorialized person. This may be as simple as just choosing a certain design on a ceramic pot that was her favorite color.

2. Go to a florist or garden center and ask for help in designing this project. Talk about where it will be located, what gardening skills might be required to keep it healthy and how best to lay it out.

3. Purchase the materials and assemble the project yourself or ask others if you need help to bring it together. Take your time with this project because each planting will afford you time to reflect on your wife and connect closer to her spirit.

4. Think about adding a time capsule. Fill it with mementos that describe your wife to the person who may find it someday. This can be easily made with PVC pipe (4" diam. 12' long) and two end caps. Your hardware store can cut this to length and supply the glue to make it watertight.

5. If your wife was interred, maintain the site seasonally and pay a visit on key dates of the year (birthday, anniversary, etc.) If ashes were dispersed at a site, cast flowers or pay a similar tribute at that location.

Journaling follow-up:

1. What specific steps can I take to create the most meaningful memorial garden in honor of my wife?
2. How do I feel when I view the natural beauty of the garden?
3. How will this memorial garden provide an ongoing tribute to my wife's life?

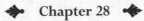

Chapter 28

Choose to Read

One of the most common messages I hear from both men and women stricken with grief is, "No one understands. I feel so alone." Understanding the root causes behind individual styles of mourning is difficult, but resources exist to help one get through it. Because everyone is an individual in how loss affects them, unique approaches to grief and loss can be helpful to both men and women and should be investigated. Some bereaved may be most comfortable discussing their grief in a support group, while others feel better served with grief education, immersion into music or performing an activity such as gardening, artistry or writing.

Reading has been found to be an effective method of easing one's grief because it provides a relaxing atmosphere for the bereaved to separate himself from his new reality without his spouse and allows him to shift his thinking to enjoyable thoughts. The opportunity to utilize his imagination to connect with fresh thoughts and places permits them to move into a world of solitude and for that moment forget about the pains associated with his loss.

After the death of a wife, the survivor's mind is constantly preoccupied with worry and the stress of surviving the transition to a life without her. This negative self-talk seems to be endless and therefore very inhibiting to the healing process and downright harmful to one's overall health. This is particularly evident when people who are grieving cannot sleep well. The physical quietness of lying in bed gives a moment of pause that allows one's inner voice of self-talk at this anguished point to be easily heard. I have found this disruptive voice can be silenced through reading just before going to sleep. Reading forces the mind to take a break from destructive self-talk and allows the mind to hear a fresh message. This works particularly well when the new message is one that is positive or comforting to the reader. Such positive comfort will give a much needed lift to the depression of grief even if it is for only a few minutes each day. Scientific studies have shown that releasing negative thoughts and replacing them with positive messages prior to falling asleep is the best way to make lasting peaceful changes to your life. You may or may not be a person who reads for pleasure, but reading when you are suffering grief over the loss of your wife can give you that much needed moment of solitude that can slow down the world around you— even if just for a short while at the end of a long day. This is provided that the choice of the literature is also conducive to relaxing the mind. For example, reading subject matter dealing with graphic violence will not serve to relaxing one's mind as compared to reading about nature. So, the most desirable subject matter is that which develops thoughts that please the reader.

***

Reading is something we do every day without thinking about it. We read stop signs, reports at our places of work and our mail. However, reading for the sake of pleasure seems to be a dying pastime. Books are turned into DVDs so quickly now that we don't even know that they were books in the first place. We scan newspapers, Web sites and billboards because something has caught our attention, then we quickly move on to the next thing.

When we read for the sake of truly understanding an author's thoughts, we use the innermost imaginative parts of our mind. We envision new and exciting places, feel the emotions of the characters or learn some new factual element of our own world. Reading puts us into a state where we hear our own familiar inner voice communicating to us the subject at hand.

***

I typically read non-fiction as I found that with little time to devote to this enjoyable pastime I wanted to insure that I could learn something to broaden my horizons. But I have since found that the books Terri read were much more stress-reducing than what I had been choosing. In Terri's final months, her choices in spiritual books gave me a deeper understanding of God's will; and, because of this newfound knowledge, I developed a sense of peace despite what was forthcoming. I also found that reading such books just prior to bedtime helped to refocus my thoughts and to turn off the negative self-talk, which means that I get better sleep. I still occasionally grab the book of spiritualism that sits on her dresser and read it before turning off the lamp.

***

"I'm not much of a reader, but with the little time I did have, I read the booklets that the funeral home had sent me. I got them every few months. It was something that I could sit down and read in one sitting. Some of the information I found helpful because they described feelings that I was having, but other things didn't necessarily fit for me either. All in all they were good for me." –Scott

***

Getting started using reading as a method to heal your grief is actually very easy to do. You are already doing just that by reading this book, but there are many more ways to have fun with this task. Try one or all of the ideas listed, and you may just find yourself rediscovering an interest that will become a lifelong endeavor.

- Read a book or magazine that your wife had read. Try to feel why your wife may have enjoyed it. Imagine what attracted her to it and what she might have said to others about it. Maybe she already told you it was her favorite book or her favorite author. If you reflect upon why your wife may have enjoyed a particular book, you may discover some deeper understanding of her values.
- Go to your library and look up books on poetry. While poetry may not be some men's usual choice, the death of a wife can bring

feelings about despair that many authors have captured quite well through the ages. Homer's *Odyssey* and Longfellow's *A Psalm of Life* are just two examples of poetic literature that have personally brought me comfort and insight. By reading such works, you will learn that others have shared the same sense of loss that you are feeling, and this sense of communion will soothe your pain through understanding.

- Share the gift of reading by donating your wife's books to a school, church or library.
- Donate a memorial gift to your local library to increase the collection of your wife's favorite subject.
- Read a spiritual passage daily. There are many guides available at religious supply or bookstores that can help you.
- Transfer your wife's magazine subscriptions to one of her friends.
- Read a joke book and share a joke with people, or select a joke you feel your wife would have laughed at and e-mail the joke to her friends.

The ideas mentioned are just a start to the many ways you can reconnect to reading as a tool to heal your loss. When grieving it is all too easy to give up on one's interests for an existence with no promise of a happier tomorrow. Lying awake at night worrying about a problem isn't moving you toward a solution and listening to your worries run incessantly through your mind isn't healthy. Instead, be preemptive. Take those few minutes before bedtime and grab a book that will fill up your emotional gas tank each night so that you can find comfort and feel better about life the next day.

Instructions:

1. Try one of the ideas or think of other ways to involve reading in your nightly ritual.
2. Read wherever and whenever you can for the pure enjoyment of it. Reading for enjoyment is a great way to bring peace to your life throughout your day.
3. Combine this activity with another chapter's ideas in learning more about your topic of choice such as exercise, diet, meditation, affirmations or scripture.

Journaling follow-up:

1. How have I incorporated reading into my daily activities as a ritual?
2. How has reading helped me to change negative thoughts into positive messages and thus make lasting, peaceful changes in my life?
3. What is a specific activity that I can perform which will incorporate my wife's reading preferences, with the goal of helping others or myself?

Chapter 29

Imagine
the Other Side

Many of you that read this book are probably already thinking, *I don't believe in psychics, the paranormal, ghosts, poltergeists, aliens, you name it—they just don't exist.* You might already be asking yourself, *What is this activity going to do for me?* While we're not going to try to convince you one way or the other, this activity may be one that gives you astonishing results and some good entertainment for you and a friend.

Some people tend to react especially critically to the idea of psychics. However, if you stop to think about it, have you ever felt that some people were more intuitive than you? Have you ever felt that some people radiate negative energy, while others radiate positive energy? Maybe you even realized this before you got to know them. Have you ever answered the phone and knew who was on the other end of the line before you said hello? Have you ever made a decision based solely on a gut feeling—and it was the right decision?

Well, if you said yes to any of these ideas, then maybe you are not quite as much of a skeptic as you thought. Here are some others to ponder. Have you ever wondered if it was possible that your wife might want to get a message through to you? Would you believe that if it were possible, your wife might want to guide you on an important decision? There are countless reports of nonbelievers who have been amazed beyond their wildest dreams from supernatural experiences after the death of their spouses. Maybe you could be next!

***

Is the Paranormal Real?

Soon after a spouse's death, the survivor often starts the grieving process wondering not only about the new journey he will be traveling but also about his deceased loved one's journey as well. It is normal to ask questions about this journey. Did your wife feel any pain before she crossed over in her last minutes of life? Did anyone from the other side greet her when she crossed over? Does she actually know how you feel and what is happening to you in your daily life? Is she happy and content now? Does she see you, and how will you know when she is around? These questions are very concerning to the bereaved and are shared by many who are looking for answers.

Paranormal experiences among the bereaved have frequently been reported. In 1975, British practitioner W. Dewi Rees interviewed 227 widows and sixty-seven widowers and found that 46.7 percent (50 percent of men and 45.8 percent of women) had had paranormal experiences related to their deceased spouses. Experiences included a sense of presence of the dead spouse (felt by 39.2 percent), visual experiences (13.3 percent), auditory experiences (13.3 percent) and speech with the deceased spouse (11.6 percent).

The bereaved often cite feeling their spouses' presence, guidance and love at various moments in their daily routines. In such cases, the feeling is sufficiently impactful enough that they also report a sense of knowing and communicating with the deceased that is routinely described as a gut feeling, but when pressed, they confide they are certain the experience is much more real. They are certain the event is much different from anything else they have ever experienced, and they are unwilling to blame it on a biochemical or other scientific cause. These experiences are so real that the bereaved find comfort in them, because they feel they will once again be reunited with their loved ones. Regardless of the root cause of the experiences, the bereaved who feel a connection to the other side are comforted by the phenomenon.

***

"If there is a hereafter, fine. If there isn't, well I'm living my life as if there is. If I'm wrong, I'll never know the difference and, if I'm right, I hope I did enough good so they'll let me in." –Jerry B.

***

As an engineer who makes a living utilizing a logical approach to probably too many aspects of my life and as a person deeply grounded in my Christian faith, I would have never in my wildest imagination thought that I would come to the conclusion I have now on this topic. In the final year prior to Terri's death, there were numerous instances of our personal prayers being directly answered. We discussed this openly and felt that not only were God and Jesus present with us through our difficult journey, but so were other family members, such as my mother who had crossed over nearly twelve years before.

After Terri's death, I had no fewer than fourteen occurrences of her contacting me in answer to specific requests of mine. These events were so powerful that they compelled me to find out more about their validity, as I knew I was under significant stress and wondered if I was force-fitting the events into the framework of a contact to appease my own mind.

I decided to contact a complete stranger over 1,200 miles away who had a well known reputation for psychic ability. Within five minutes of performing a reading for me, he mentioned numerous specific facts that there was no possibility of him knowing prior to the contact. One example was a direct quote of a favorite phrase my deceased sister-in-law frequently used. This was just one of several examples that validated the contact for me as being real. All I can suggest is that you try it and let your own heart and mind decide.

This activity does not have to conflict with any beliefs you may hold to be true. I personally believe that God allows our loved ones to comfort those left behind and may even use these communications to help bolster our belief and understanding as to why our loved ones needed to cross over when they did.

***

"One time I was sleeping in bed and I suddenly awoke with my hand outstretched feeling that Kathy was holding my hand. I'm not certain if it was a dream or something else, but I did find it comforting. I will tell you that I talk to Kathy every day. I guess I do it because it helps me feel better about making decisions now and other thoughts I think she would have an influence on." –Rick

***

"My friend Dean, whom my wife, Marge, and I have known for many years, called me up one day and said that Marge came to him in a dream. He said that in the dream, Marge said, 'Tell Joe I'm okay.' It really impacted me, because I had been finding it difficult to go and visit her grave site. I drove by and talked to her as I did so, but I could never pull my car in to visit it. Then, several weeks later, without knowing about my friend Dean's story, my girlfriend told me Marge came to her in a dream. She said that I was driving my car with Marge and her in the backseat. Marge said to my girlfriend, 'I'm okay with this.' So you tell me how two independent people can have such powerful dreams about two key issues that I have been concerned about; me wondering about Marge's spirit and if dating was acceptable to her? I'm not questioning it." –Joe

***

If you are hesitant about whether paranormal experiences may conflict with your religious background, take the time to meet with your spiritual leader to discuss his or her opinions and evidence for the other side. Tap into his or her knowledge on the subject and draw your own conclusions. If you are still struggling with how the concept of the supernatural may fit into your belief systems, why not approach this with the simple purpose of learning more about the subject and what others believe.

Instructions:

1. Go to your library or local bookstore and read books and articles on communication with the other side to build your understanding as to why people believe in it.

2. Research local psychics. Call them and ask for references. Call these references and ask about their original belief system and how it might have changed since visiting a psychic. Ask them if they are willing to share why they went to one.

3. There are many psychic/wellness fairs around the country. Search the Web to discover local events where you can learn more. They can be very reasonable in cost and can offer a variety of books and other information on the subject matter. Some offer readings at the shows.

4. Set up an appointment for a personal reading and ask if you should bring anything or prepare in any way for the reading. Go to the reading with a recording device and record the reading. If you do not have a recorder, bring a friend to take notes as the reading progresses. Do not discuss any subject with the psychic before the reading takes place. During the reading, do not lead the reader, but let the person do the talking. If asked a question, a simple yes or no should be sufficient. The best psychics actually prefer it that way so they can further refine and understand their own experiences.

5. Play back the recording and discuss with a friend the validity of the information and how to interpret it.

Journaling follow-up:

1. What research or personal contact have I done to help educate myself on the topic of psychic ability?

2. What are my personal beliefs about the authenticity and possible benefit of experiencing contact with those who have crossed over?

3. What experiences have I had, if any, in which I felt my wife had a presence or direct influence on a life event or decision? What was my reaction to this experience?

Chapter 30

Keep Memories
in Motion

We collect images through photographs, family movies or simple renderings from art class in school to preserve moments in our lives. These images help us remember past events. We also look at them as defining moments in the lives we share with each other. Past snapshots of you and your wife from your dating days to the present, as well as with your family, become especially significant when she passes away.

This exercise honors your wife by collecting the best imagery of her life and putting it on a disc. Once on a CD or DVD, the disc can be easily duplicated and shared with family and friends. This activity can be a lasting tribute to her life, preserved by a medium that is durable and easily distributed. If done soon enough, this tribute can be played at the funeral or celebration of life service so others can recall what a wonderful relative or friend they had.

***

Roll 'Em

Tom reflects, "During one particular group counseling session, a widower, his two children and two grandchildren reflected on the powerful experience of creating a DVD of their wife, mother and grandmother, which they used during her wake service and funeral. They demonstrated the full range of emotions from intense grief and tearfulness to joy and laughter as they found the benefit of creating the DVD as a powerful means of reflecting on her life and the joy that she brought to her family and others."

Due to the effects of grieving, the aging process or a variety of other potentially troublesome factors in life, it becomes difficult to recall the variety of memories created by one's spousal relationship. The creation of a DVD of a loved one is a highly effective way to fulfill one's need to retain visual images of the life and the memories that you shared together.

***

I was fortunate enough to have developed such a synopsis of our twenty-year marriage in a DVD lasting twenty minutes. We wanted to make Terri's funeral a celebration of her life and really create the feeling that she had given us. The numerous positive responses I received about her video assured me that it was a great tribute to her and that other people appreciated one lasting image of her.

A digital DVD has the many benefits of being a mixture of media: slide show, video and audio. The options are endless. Favorite photos of your wife can be layered with music that was meaningful to her or the both of you. Videotape from past trips such as your honeymoon and family vacations can be spliced into the disk. You can even ask her employer for photos or other media she may have for inclusion into this DVD. Do this particularly if her job had her in front of a camera.

***

"I have a ton of 8mm video tape of Marnie and the family. But something happened to my camera and it doesn't work anymore. I can't play the tapes. I really have to find some way of getting all those moments captured onto a DVD so I can preserve them and be able to watch them again. Her dad would just love it if I could give him a DVD of movies with her in them." –Ross

***

Remembering the finer details of your wife's character is made much easier when you create a vivid means of documenting the memories of her life. The film is a great way to review her life on anniversaries and other important dates. Be sure to store this collection of images in your memory box (see chapter 12) for future use.

Instructions:

1. Sort through family videos, photos, artwork, audio tracks and any other media that includes your loved one. A good assortment of items from her work, leisure hobbies and family time works best. Ask family, friends and even her employer for any media that might define events that you weren't directly a participant in but that helped define her life.

2. Look in the phonebook under videography or photography services. Many photo shops can refer you to a person in the area who does video editing. Make an appointment to review the ideas and the wide range of options they can produce for you. If you are talented enough, many computer stores offer fairly low cost hardware that can easily download videotape into a digital format, let you edit it and then burn a DVD. Ask your computer savvy friends for help in this area. Many young men and women, especially those with children, now record and edit digital video and have this equipment readily available. This sort of assistance when planning a celebration of life service is highly valuable—so ask.

3. Record the disc and make note of who would like a copy. Make up the discs and labels ahead of time as you may want to give these as memorials at the service. Remember to make enough only for those who might get use out of it long after the first viewing. If you simply do not have the time or the will to have them ready at your wife's funeral, give them out at a later date.

Journaling follow-up:

1. What steps have I taken to collect and organize the various forms of media, which represent my wife's life?

2. What range of emotions did I feel as I was reminiscing while using these items?

3. How has the use of this media provided me with a positive means for others and myself to return to the memories of my wife's life?

Chapter 31

Find a
New Best Friend

Sometimes the death of a wife leaves the survivor alone in the home. The large shift from being needed by someone to being needed by no one is often the hardest of all heartaches to bear. Walking into an empty home after a long day at work with no sense of purpose for another can truly be the most difficult change one experiences. This is especially true the longer that you and your wife were together. If your relationship was built on a solid foundation, you may feel that you couldn't conceive a full life prior to marriage and now you cannot conceive life without your spouse. While there is no substitute for a longtime companion, there are ways that this sort of pain can be eased.

One way to greatly reduce these feelings is to purchase a pet! The mere presence of a new and lively spirit in the house, with the unconditional love that a pet provides, will give your own spirit a boost. People who previously owned pets will understand the benefits that they can provide. Select a pet that can fit easily into your lifestyle. Consider where you live and nearby facilities that would be conducive to the pet's happiness. This pet can be something as simple as a fish, a rat (yes...rats make great pets), a cat or a dog.

***

Only My Dog Understands Me

Men have been found to engage in secret grief, a method of solitary mourning activity, in which they purposely withdraw from others while grieving in order to spare others from seeing, feeling or experiencing their grief. Men who gravitate toward secret grief view the alternative public expression of grief as a direct violation of the males' cultural expectation related to grieving, which reiterates that big boys don't cry.

Men who engage in secret grief may obtain pets and find the pets are their new best friends and a safe means of relieving that grief. This is especially true as they engage in private activities such as going for a walk or car ride alone. Tom encourages men to embrace opportunities to share their new pets with those around them. They represent *new life*, unconditional love and a much needed, renewed sense of companionship. Men who are grieving the losses of their spouses are yearning to fill the need to be needed. Adopting a pet can be a vital first step in helping fulfill this critical need and heighten one's sense of self worth.

***

"We had a Schnauzer for seven years named Nubbs that Mickey had picked out. I guess since her family had Schnauzers, that's why we ended up with one. Unfortunately only a few months after Mickey died, Nubbs died. It felt like two kicks to the gut, because a dog can feel like a family member, too. So we got another dog—Louie—and there was never a doubt that he would be a Schnauzer, too. Getting Louie brought a lot of fun and laughter back into our house when we needed it most. He's somebody to love, to fill a void and put a smile on our faces." –Mark

***

Due to our busy work schedules and more importantly to our pet allergies, we never owned a cat or dog, and there was no way a rat would ever have lived under the same roof as Terri! However, I can relate to people who feel a deep connection to their pets. Even in my limited exposure to other people's animals, I know that I really enjoy giving creatures their much deserved attention. They seem to take an immediate liking to me and I easily take to them. Maybe it's because deep down

I know I won't be bringing them home with me, and I therefore won't have to worry about who will take care of their needs while I am at work! I truly enjoy the uplifting and endless sense of love they radiate to people. A pet's unconditional love cannot be underestimated.

Seriously consider owning a pet when you are adjusting to the increased workload of living without your wife. However, pets require a commitment from their owners so that they are properly cared for and loved in return, so do not make this decision hastily. Remember, you want to make this a positive experience and lasting partnership for you and your pet. If you do decide to do this activity, then consider:

- How much time you have to devote to the care of the pet. Think about how your lifestyle will fit with your pet. Fish require less work than a dog for example, but you won't have the added benefits of a walking partner or someone that can jump on your lap while you watch television.

- How much you can afford to spend. Smaller pets cost less to purchase, maintain and feed. Consider the pet's health costs since it is not uncommon for veterinarian bills to be several hundred dollars for common illnesses.

- If the pet will be compatible with all family members and with the home environment that you will provide. Do your homework and ask knowledgeable people for advice before making the commitment to an animal that may not have the temperament to thrive in your home and family.

- Alternative sources to obtain your pet such as the local animal shelter or through a neighbor or co-worker who may be giving away an animal. Often, local newspapers have ads that will be offering a pet for free to a good home. Ask around and you might just be saving an animal from being destroyed.

- Finally, after you have gained good advice, prepare your home and the animal for a good start together. Insure the proper health checks such as vaccinations and other preparations are in place before you become emotionally attached to an animal that may need serious medical and financial resources. You might be able to try the pet for a few hours before taking permanent ownership so that you are assured of a good match.

Once you have made the decision to own a pet, the fun is just beginning! Give your new friend a name that has significant connection to your deceased's memory. Maybe there was a pet you previously shared and you can brainstorm and create a name similar to that animal. Think of what your wife might have named the pet if she were to have been given the task or refer to her hobbies or interests as a starting point for picking a name. For example, maybe your wife was a good seamstress and your animal of choice is a Russian Blue cat you name Stitch!

Your decision is an important one when it involves the life of a creature and should not be taken lightly. Be certain that your decision is carefully made with all the considerations mentioned, and you are on your way to a lasting friendship for years to come.

Instructions:

1. Seek out information from the library or Internet on a variety of pets that you might be considering. Do your homework so that you make a lasting choice that you will treasure and never forget.
2. Investigate options on where you can find your pet. This may be the humane society, newspaper or a pet store. Sea Monkeys only count if you are on a budget!
3. Give your pet a name and be creative in the process with a contest with close friends or similar idea or just follow these suggestions.

Journaling follow-up:

1. What potential animals would be a great match for me and my family and why?
2. What factors do I need to consider as I try to determine if and when I am ready for a pet, with regards to the emotional impact and the degree of commitment required?
3. How will a pet provide me with a renewed sense of being needed?

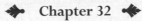# Chapter 32

Harbor No
More Regrets

With the loss of a wife, it is almost a certainty to have feelings of regret. Important topics never discussed, unfulfilled promises and lost opportunities are thoughts that can bring on feelings of extreme sadness. These feelings are particularly painful, because they are often rooted in memories of times where we were not at our best with our spouses. We berate ourselves because of minor events when we failed to act in accordance with our deepest desires, because it was easier to choose a simpler path. After our spouses are gone, we reflect on those moments where we could have made a difference, if we had simply chosen to be more supportive of their requests, given them more attention when they needed it or maybe even just simply said "I love you" more than we did.

The unfulfilled promises and lost opportunities are relatively easier to forgive as these choices involved our spouse's acceptance to some degree of the path that was chosen. Both of you allowed the decision to be made the way it was, you each had some responsibility for the direction taken and you both lived with the result. For these joint miscues, we need to quickly forgive ourselves and move on.

The regret about thoughts left unsaid, however, is a much more complex issue to resolve and from which to move forward. I believe that feeling regret for thoughts left unsaid is a significant barrier to achieving inner peace for the surviving widower. We wonder if we may have been too assuming of our relationships and if we ever articulated the depth of love and appreciation we felt for our spouses. Did we choose to avoid conflict by not sharing our deepest core thoughts on an important issue, while leaving key decisions to fall solely on our spouses? Should we have offered them more support even though they may not have directly asked for it? Take a moment and think about how a simple act of hugging and giving thanks while a spouse performed an everyday task is now an opportunity lost forever. What would it have cost us to have done more of this while they were with us? It was our choice not to communicate this appreciation to them.

There are many reasons behind the feelings of regret we harbor after losing a wife. We worry that we did not actively communicate love for them, we did not offer enough words of encouragement or support on a difficult issue, we did not seek to understand their viewpoint and sometimes we were not good listeners. Whatever the reason behind the regret, we can still make amends now.

***

Real Men Don't Ask for Directions

In some form or another, we all have some amount of regret. No one is perfect. Sometimes an imperfect life with one's spouse can leave the bereaved feeling that there is unfinished business, and it is not always easy to let go of those imperfect moments. Forgiveness for yourself, your deceased spouse or even those associated with your spouse, is a necessary part of healing. It is also a process. You can make up your mind that you need to forgive, but it sometimes isn't as easy as just deciding that it's the right thing to do. It may take quite a while to completely forgive yourself or the other person. The process, however, is an important one because letting go of past mistakes is a foundation stone in the healing process on which the bereaved can build a new life.

Don't try to forgive too soon in your grief process. You have to go through the anger and the guilt and work through both thoroughly before you can forgive. Forgiveness for both you and your spouse is required in order for you to heal. To forgive is to do it for you, not the other person. Forgiveness is very freeing, and it is necessary in order for you to get on with your life without regret.

Men and women in Tom's grief group report very distinct differences with regards to their specific sources of regret. While widows often speak of feeling abandoned or deserted, widowers tend to express the loss as one of "dismemberment," as if they had lost something that kept them organized and whole. Men often equate the death of their wives with the loss of their primary source of protection, support and comfort. This is at the very core of their overall sense of well-being. One widower described his experience as "being lost without a compass," typically due to his extreme loneliness, but also because he depended on his wife for many things like managing the household, caring for their children and being his only true confidant. This sense of regret and being lost is even more esoteric as this particular widower reported needing help but experienced difficulty obtaining or even asking for it. He also reported experiencing ambiguity about the emotions he was feeling and the uncertainty of how to express them.

***

In our final days together, I felt an overwhelming need to communicate as much as I could with Terri. My intent was to connect with her on as many levels as possible to extract all of her thoughts to carry me for the rest of my life. Many of the subjects were simply too painful to openly discuss, so I wrote them in a hardcover journal for Terri to read. I mention this example several times in this book for very good reason. This was a very powerful and final step we took in ending our Earthly life together. Sharing our innermost thoughts and feelings in that journal sealed the relationship we shared. I added to that journal almost every day and I knew she was reading it. Some of the thoughts were quite serious and yet others were memories of happier times and the meaning she put into my life. Unfortunately, I ran out of time with Terri and I felt the journal needed a closing chapter. I wrote some final thoughts, pulling together the promises that I made, the importance of Terri's life to me and that we would someday meet again in one final entry. In the end, while very healing for me, that book was for her—a keepsake of sorts. The value of this exercise culminated when I was asked by the funeral director if we had anything to be cremated with her. I gave him the journal. I feel these thoughts are with Terri now even more strongly than before when she read those pages.

You can bring closure to the relationship you had with your wife even now after her death. Think about getting closure on *all* the emotions you feel about your relationship. Be sure to cover any feelings of regret or guilt, but don't forget to include the positive feelings of gratitude that you wish to communicate with your wife. Shed these strong feelings by getting them down on paper and out in the open. Like other tasks in this book, the hardest part may be in beginning the process.

Find a comfortable place where you can sit down undisturbed and gather your thoughts about the relationship you had with your wife. Think about the times when you were not at your best with her and jot down some notes that would describe the situation, your perspective of it and the position held by your wife. For this exercise to have meaning, keep in mind that you do not have to recall every last detail of every instance that you feel you reacted incorrectly during all the years you knew each other. The intent is to capture key themes by selecting a few examples from the past, so that you can better record the issues in your writing that you want resolved in your heart. Now that you have a few examples to draw from, the simplest way to gain resolution is to kick start your writing by completing this simple sentence:

"I regret that I _____ because it did not _____ and so it resulted in _____."

Feel free to use this line over and over, for all the areas you feel you want to clarify. If the format line is not your style, just start writing a letter based upon your reflections. No format is better than the other, just do what feels best and easiest for you to complete. You may then choose to conclude your letter by reflecting on what the relationship meant to you and how you feel about your future. Once your letter is complete, you may wish to set it aside for a day or two and then revisit it to confirm that you have covered all the issues that resound in your heart. Feel free to add to the letter, but eventually you will come to realize it covers all that needs to be said and is complete. Next, think of a way how you can permanently give the letter up to symbolize the resolution of these thoughts and the forgiveness you seek from your wife. You could burn, bury or even cast it into water, but regardless, be sure to surrender the letter to your wife so that the energy that surrounds the letter is released from you. In this way, you can now rest knowing that you have gained closure on the open issues that previously racked your mind.

This exercise forces us to become aware of and then reflect on the undercurrent of our subconscious. By doing so, we can clearly acknowledge these painful thoughts, and then ask for our spouses and God to forgive and heal us. By acknowledging where we strayed and asking for forgiveness, we can begin to forgive ourselves.

***

"I don't have any regrets about my relationship with Robin, but I will say I sometimes feel regret when I can't find time to spend with my boys. I have a full-time job, a side business and I run the household, which leaves little time for me to spend with them. This bothers me a lot and it has been a struggle. When I do get new work, I constantly have to evaluate if I want the work or to spend time with my boys. I have given a lot of work to my competition. I do remind myself though that I can't feel regret for the things I can't control." —Scott

***

The Road That Has Made All the Difference

In Scott's situation, we see a different struggle with feelings of regret as he attempts to maintain a healthy balance between his work responsibilities and his desire to preserve time with his sons. It is admirable to see Scott's efforts to acknowledge potential sources of regret, while coming to a sincere peace of mind with the choices he continues to face in his life. Scott appears to be making positive strides in accepting the reality that he will face situations certainly out of his control, which is a critical component of letting go of past and current regrets.

***

Instructions:

1. Take a moment in your favorite place to relax and think back on your life with your wife. Recall the moments when you feel that you:
   a. Let your wife down and did not deliver on a commitment
   b. Avoided discussing something that was important to her
   c. Did not listen
   d. Did not tell her you loved her when she needed it
   e. Did not support her in something she wanted to do
   f. Became verbally abusive to her
   g. Feel any other form of regret
2. Now, capture those thoughts by writing them down in the simple format sentence described or start writing a letter expressing your thoughts and see where that may take you!
3. Once you have captured the thoughts, read through them to really see why you behaved the way you did. Ask yourself if it makes sense to you to continue to feel guilt over those moments. Write at the very end of the document that you ask for forgiveness and that you need to forgive yourself so that you can move past your grief.
4. After you are satisfied that you can release or forgive yourself for the moments that are giving you regret, destroy the document by burning it, burying it, etc. This symbolizes that the hardships have now evaporated and a clean slate has been established between you and your wife.

Journaling follow-up:

1. What feelings of regret do I continue to harbor since the death of my wife?
2. How have these feelings of regret affected my ability to feel healed and forgiven, both by my wife and by myself?
3. In addition to asking for forgiveness, what specific steps can I take to help release the guilt and grief that I have felt?

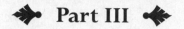

Part III

Giving Back
to Others

"Help thy brother's boat across and lo
thine own has reached the shore."
Hindu Proverb

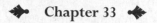

Chapter 33

Show
Gratitude

When a wife dies, many people come to our aid in many different ways. Some assist us significantly with their actions, while others do small things for us, but the reason for their help is always the same: They have empathy for the bereaved. They act on whatever they think will be of assistance to us and what they can personally contribute in order to make our grief more bearable.

Some survivors forget who helped them the most, before the emotional support from family and friends arrives. It is easy to overlook the people who may have had direct contact with your deceased wife very near her time of passing or shortly thereafter. Assistance may have been provided by doctors, nurses, police, firefighters and emergency medical technicians to name a few examples. These people may include those who cared for the individual such as in-home nursing personnel or other supportive living personnel. During the time of bereavement, the funeral director, cemetery personnel and support staff are sure to have helped the family in making decisions. So in your desire to show gratitude, be aware that the people who may have helped your wife include others beside those who attended the funeral service or visited afterward.

***

Mean It Like You Say It

Saying thank you is not so tough for most people, but modeling the true spirit of gratitude takes much more effort. The fast pace of today's society has in many ways created an increased sense of entitlement. Sometimes we get so focused on our rights that we forget to be gracious and appreciative of what we really do possess. Modeling gratitude is helpful to anyone's sense of happiness—bereaved or not. When we are gracious, an awareness of appreciating small everyday experiences occurs.

So, why is showing gratitude such an important skill to develop? Frustration comes from unmet expectations, but gratitude results in not having expectations and truly finding the happiness in whatever comes your way. Thus, living more often in such a positive state of mind will attract others to you and improve your attitude and perspective on life as a whole. Widowers who are able to find and appreciate the small things in life cite this clear and positive effect on their quality of life. Not surprisingly, this is not only good for healing grief, but also for a life-long mindset.

***

I was personally very moved by the amount of support I received from many of the service providers mentioned. Even though these were their professions and they perform such tasks on a daily basis, some took extra steps beyond their responsibilities to ensure that Terri and I knew they were empathetic. Terri passed away almost two years after her first oncologist retired. Yet, he attended her funeral to pay his respects. In his professional specialty, funerals unfortunately are common. However, he made it a point to show that extra bit of support; in doing so, he did something that I will never forget. It is the character of such people that makes the rough road of grieving much smoother, and such gestures should be recognized.

The more you practice giving thanks, the easier it is to do. Giving thanks also makes one more aware of the depth of the relationships they encounter on a daily basis. Often in our work, we are not thanked for just doing the job, but when a mention of gratitude comes directly our way, it improves our day as well as that of the person who offered it.

***

"I sent a number of thank you cards out for the many meals people brought us soon after Mickey's death. Losing my wife has changed me a lot, particularly in how I see my relationships with others. It seems as if you become more in tune to wanting to help people out and to be more aware and grateful for what others have done for you." —Mark

***

Make a list of all the people or service entities that assisted you when you needed help the most. Think about specific acts they did for you and about what their assistance meant to your life at that difficult time. If you imagine yourself as the representative of your wife saying what she would have wanted to say, then the thank you note will be that much more rewarding and therapeutic to you. Reflecting on the influence your wife had on you should develop your sense of gratitude quite easily. Just share what she would have said if given the chance.

Once you have taken the time to share your thanks with those who assisted you in your time of need, turn this new sense of gratitude into daily practice. Make an affirmation of three things to be thankful for and repeat it every morning, noon and night before retiring. Affirming gratitude daily will cause you to refocus on priorities to which you should direct your energy and the relationships with those around you. See chapter 10, "Use Affirmations", for more information.

You can show your gratitude to others in many diverse ways. Examples to consider include:

- Send the person a thank-you card, including a brief message noting the impact he or she had on you and your wife.
- Drop by and pay the person an unexpected visit just to say thanks. There is no better way to show gratitude than to take the time out of one's day and make personal contact to convey this message.
- Send flowers with a short note the florist can attach. Flowers brighten everyone's day.
- Send the person a gift card to a local coffee shop for a latte or similar small cost item.

Instructions:

1. Make a list of those who were kind to you and your wife if you over-looked giving thanks to them. Choose an idea from those mentioned or create one of your own that can convey how meaningful their actions were to you. Complete the list and enjoy a new sense of sat-isfaction of speaking for your wife in this important act of closure.

2. Add gratitude to your daily activities through affirmations or in con-veying thanks to a specific individual with whom you interact on a daily basis. Make a point to see how your relationship changes as a result of your attention to making your appreciation known to the person.

Journaling follow-up:

1. Who were the people who assisted me and my wife, either in caring for her or in offering support after she passed away?

2. What specific acts of kindness had the greatest impact on my wife and me, and why do these acts have a special meaning for me now?

3. Taking my wife's character into consideration, what are the most meaningful ways I can show gratitude toward others?

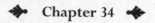

Chapter 34

Do a
Good Turn

A piece of rope with a knot in it is part of the Boy Scouts of America's national symbol. It signifies the phrase that all scouts try to live by every day—"Do a Good Turn." It reminds all who wear the emblem that their primary focus is to be in the service of others. Such a phrase stirs images of a scout helping a little old lady across the street, but as you are probably aware, scouting goes far beyond that in its efforts to build a better community. One of the most striking things about their assistance is that while they have a significant impact on the communities they serve, this impact is made through *simple* acts of assistance. They do not provide skills unique to a profession, nor do they carry with them exorbitant amounts of financial backing. They just get out there and do what needs to be done.

This chapter shows you how you can expand the positive impact you can have by assisting individuals and even larger groups of people. As the Boy Scouts use their basic skills and are effective in changing others' worlds for the better, you can also change the world for many more people than you ever dreamt possible.

How many times did your wife just do what needed to be done? The likely answer is something to the effect of too many to count. As a true partner, your wife lent a helping hand when you needed it by physically sharing the workload, providing you with emotional support and encouragement when you were feeling down and in many other enumerable ways. Now, stop and think about how she helped family, friends, social groups and others in addition to you. The magnitude of her life can become even more significant to you when you see the direct impact she had on other people beyond her immediate relationships. Now that she is gone, it is logical to wonder how you and the others she affected are ever going to heal from the loss of such a dependable supporter.

As a father of two scouts, one an Eagle Scout and the other well on his way to becoming one, I can assure you that the core value of being helpful is one that guides them towards more meaningful relationships with others. Young people may groan a bit when they must choose between fulfilling a commitment to the annual food drive for the local food pantry versus going to the movies with friends, but once they get started, they quickly realize they are fortunate to have food and they feel more personally rewarded than they would if they had just sat in a movie theater. This servitude to the community goes a long way in building a better tomorrow for the recipients as well as the volunteers. The food drive has become such a rewarding experience for our family that we find it very hard not to participate in it year after year.

Lending a hand to your community in need is a great way to embrace the sphere of influence your wife had on others and to fill the void she left behind. You could call this help "giving back to society" or "paying it forward." No antidepressant or amount of money can give you the intrinsic reward that comes from helping others. Your experience in dealing with the loss of your wife can, by itself, make you a resource to others. The unique perspective of your experiences, like dealing with the negligence of others or maybe comforting your wife through the stages of a terminal illness, can guide you in helping others dealing with similar situations.

***

"The biggest thing I ever got from Kathy was the inspiration and drive to help other people. We started a charitable foundation called 'Ribbon of Hope' with two other breast cancer survivors to support those affected by the disease and I am still an active member of the foundation. The foundation helps women in many ways on a local level such as paying for co-pays that many women cannot afford. We went from a first year budget of only $20,000 to giving out over half a million dollars in six short years. By being directly involved, I can see firsthand how I am helping individuals and making a difference. I'm in awe of what four people initially set out to do and where the foundation is today. They'll have to kick me out before I will ever leave!" –Rick

***

The Way Things Work

Males are conditioned early on to believe they can build or fix anything. They surround themselves with the necessary tools and skills to be able to complete the task at hand. The ability to succeed in completing a task provides them with a sense of purpose and self worth. Many widowers have experienced heart-wrenching feelings of helplessness due to their inability to "fix" their spouses' terminal illnesses.

Through the act of reaching out to help others during their grief, men experience compassion as they aide others in need and ease their life's challenges, even if done in a very simple way. The act of providing a good turn to another offers an equal, if not greater, impact on men in grief, as this act re-instills the lifelong need to feel as though they have the ability to fix some aspect of another's life, thus providing a renewed sense of purpose, meaning and self worth.

Men often find themselves in awe of their deceased spouses as they reflect on their wives' unending abilities to reach out to others and live a life of service and compassion. Men often feel they don't measure up to these abilities in such softer skills of kindness and compassion. However, by embracing these characteristics of their spouses and emulating these behaviors, they become more connected to the memory of what defined their relationships and ultimately more comfortable through this new-found understanding.

A local hospice staff reported to me that several men whose wives received hospice care became involved in volunteering after their wives had passed away. They viewed this service of volunteering as their way of giving back to the hospice organization and to those patients and family members who benefit from their support. They felt indebted for the support they received during their wives' illnesses and thus felt a need to do a good turn.

***

Here is a diverse list of ideas for helping others. Pick a favorite activity and see where it takes you:

- Volunteer at your local hospital. They have many opportunities to serve such as transporting patients, parking cars, providing assistance in prepping patients for tests and procedures and so forth. Even reading books or playing games with children in the pediatric ward provides a service to others in need.
- Volunteer at your nearest hospice center. Hospice provides many benefits for an individual suffering the pending loss of a terminally ill loved one. Your presence can be a comfort to someone who is facing the loss of a loved one.
- Volunteer with an annual charitable fundraiser. These are numerous and varied. Maybe your profession can provide a skill much needed by them such as promotional advertising or run/walk coordination as a few examples. Make a call and find out.
- Help finance a charity. You may find that at this moment, your days are filled to capacity and volunteering just won't fit into your schedule. If you have no time to volunteer, make it a point to donate financially to a charity of your choice.
- Create an informational pamphlet. Maybe you do not have the ongoing time to help. In this case, think about providing a literary resource that can help many people down the road as in the development of an information pamphlet on a specific topic. Bring this reference to the leadership of a charity or clinic and explain how the information has helped you and how you brought all of these sources to one reference guide. Give this document or computer file to them for ongoing use. You might want to place a dedication statement on it to pay tribute to the memory of your wife.

- Create an all-in-one reference manual. Review any information you might have collected in your experience (literature resources, websites, political contacts, useful DVD and audio CD titles, charities, companies, etc) and reorganize it into a primer that can be easily given to aid another. Sometimes just providing information collected from numerous sources into a binder can be a tremendous help to someone.

- Use your professional skills. Analyze what skills or network of resources you personally have and how they might possibly translate to assisting someone. Summarize these skills into a document not unlike a resume of sorts or even make up a homemade business card on your PC that you can give to people in need as you meet them.

- Be a spokesperson or life example for a charity. Offer your experience for use in promoting a charity or action group's message to the public. If your wife was killed tragically by a drunk driver or by some other violent means, you may feel that a message for change to society is warranted. For instance, your "story" on a billboard or in an announcement could make a difference.

- Challenge a student to effect some change. Sponsor a scholarship in your wife's name and advertise the criteria, which will be used to determine the winner. Make a requirement that highlights the need for a change in society's outlook on a particular problem. Your local high school, technical school or college would probably be glad to help you with this project. Ensure the scholarship is done in your wife's name and advertised as such. When awarded to the recipient, you may choose to give the award in a forum that allows for you to publically call attention to the need for increased community support for your chosen cause. This can be done at an all school assembly for example, so just ask and leverage this moment to get your message out while taking delight in furthering a person's education.

**

"Mickey's sister established an annual scholarship fund at the local high school for $500 in her memory. It has nothing to do with academics or athletics and any student can apply for it. It's really designed around finding a student who has a zest for life. The applicants have to write an essay on why their qualifications and lifestyle demonstrates living life to the fullest. We feel Mickey personified this exuberance in life and she was always willing to help anyone regardless of their need." –Mark

***

Finding a way to affect a larger group of people by volunteering your skills is easier than it might first seem. Most, if not all, charities and volunteer organizations have workloads that far exceed their manpower resources required to get the work done. The charities that help people in various types of difficulties or stages of grief are numerous. Start by contacting a charity that personifies your own message or that you feel connected to in some way. Discuss with them your experiences, skills and knowledge, and ask how they feel you might best be utilized in their organization. Alternatively, you might want to come right out and ask about a specific task or skill you would like to employ for them. Either way, you just might find a position you will enjoy for a very long time.

Instructions:
1. Try one or more of the ideas mentioned, or be creative and develop your own idea that will allow you to help larger groups of people who could benefit from your skills and experience.

Journaling follow-up:
1. What is one community group or activity I can embrace as a means of helping others?
2. What impact did providing a lending hand to others have on me?
3. How has my involvement in my community help raise an awareness of the influence my wife had on others and my efforts to continue her legacy?

Chapter 35

Develop a
Product with a Cause

When our spouses pass on, we are left with substantial periods of time that would have previously been spent with them. Whether it was just a phone call or two during the workday, routine daily interactions or special times together or with our family, the void feels quite large to the grieved. We all have experienced the effect of being so busy that we lose all track of time. Conversely, when we are bored or uninvolved, the tasks seem more difficult and harder to finish in a reasonable amount of time, and the quality of the result seems to suffer. This vacant time reminds us of the emptiness we now have, and our life feels much more barren. Your task for this chapter is to fill in these voids of moments that you would have spent with your wife with an activity that honors her memory.

If we can engage ourselves in an activity that we can do either alone or with other people, we will first fill our period of sorrow with the opportunity to be productive and the possibility of even developing a new or better relationship with others. On a higher level, if the activity can somehow be tied to your deceased wife, you can feel an increased sense of connection to her while you participate in the new activity. You might ask yourself, *Even if I found the time, what can I offer people that will help others as well as myself?* You will find that once you get started, the answers become readily apparent. The key is to just start. We all have some skill that can greatly assist another. The skill can be in providing a service or a product that others would appreciate. There are many needy people in your community who could use your helping hand. Utilizing your skill will become a therapeutic experience for feeling better! Doing so will turn the unproductive time of grieving alone at home into a beneficial experience for others!

***

Take Two and Call Me in the Morning

Two widowers who knew each other joined Tom's grief group about the same time. They each talked about the love and involvement both their wives had for a local Girl Scout troop. They also shared their passion for their long time hobby of woodworking and how therapeutic it was for them. They soon developed an idea in which they joined together to build a variety of yard ornaments and household items. Then, these men donated these woodcraft items to the troop for a fundraiser with these items as prizes.

The efforts by these men provided them with a deeper sense of connection with their spouses through the ongoing fundraising activities with the troop. They were able to develop a strong sense of benevolence, while helping a cause their wives loved. Their affection for woodworking helped to fill the void of empty time and lost companionship.

***

Terri's closest friends crafted hundreds of beaded jewelry bracelets with pink beads and charms to support breast cancer victims. The bracelets were sold throughout the school where she taught. It was a very successful venture. As money was collected for the initial batch of bracelets sold, profits funded the operation for more supplies. What started out as three women with an idea resulted in several hundred dollars raised to support a local breast cancer charity and to pay for a cleaning service for our home while Terri and I were visiting hospitals and undergoing tests. This was a great help to us when we needed it most. It meant a lot to us, knowing that their energy was focused on supporting Terri and others stricken with cancer.

***

"My good friend Erik set up a benefit fund in Marnie's name prior to her death. He knew we were spending a lot of money on her treatments and wanted to help. Our friends were specific that the monies be used for the family to relax and spend quality time together—they still had hope that Marnie would pull through."–Ross

***

To get started, first identify what time commitments you can easily fit into your schedule. Keep in mind here that you are simply replacing portions of the free time you had shared with your wife. Save some of the remaining time for other activities you might be doing found elsewhere in this book. Start slowly, for example by devoting a few hours on a Friday night when you used to go to the movies together, but now you find yourself sitting at home alone. What I found to work best was doing an activity that I could fit into my schedule that had the least impact on other commitments. That is, I worked when it was convenient for me. For instance, I spent a lot of my time making repairs at our church. It provided a great service to the church and I could do the repairs at any hour of the day or night when it was most convenient for me. If you have children, consider involving them in this activity as well to fill the missing void they are feeling.

Identify what skill or knowledge you can use that would be helpful to others. Service skills such as accounting, gardening, home repairs and the like are highly valued by those who don't have those skills. Hobbies such as woodworking or knitting, creating stained glass, even stamping, scrap-booking or card making can be greatly appreciated by others. Maybe you have crafted something that others have admired. Your hobby can be a good source for an idea on what you could do for others while getting pleasure out of doing it as well! Knitted caps, key chains and beaded bracelets are all great examples of some things that can be done at a low cost while still having worth to another.

Once a skill or a product is identified, the next step is to tie it to the memory of your loved one. If your wife suffered from a disease, the items could be sold at a fundraiser to raise money for research on that disease. If your wife was affiliated with education, the funds could be used to establish a scholarship in her memory. Maybe the items could simply be donated as a tribute to your lost loved one and given away to people grieving for the same cause of death as you experienced. You may even include a small card indicating the purpose behind the item that you made.

When first considering it, this activity may seem to be too overwhelming as you struggle to develop a sense of peace in your life. Be aware the intent here is not to turn you into a superhero with unending energy to save the world; its purpose is to redirect your idle time by finding an activity that allows you to serve others. Even if you just help someone in a small way, you leave two lives a little bit better than you found them.

You may feel such a high level of intrinsic reward in performing the activities in this chapter that you may want to do more for the people you choose to help. For suggestions on reaching influence in helping charitable causes, refer to chapter 34, "Do a Good Turn".

***

"We set up a memorial that raised $15,000 for Ribbon of Hope. The Ribbon of Hope also started a new program at Christmas called Kathy's Christmas Gift of Hope. This giving program designates five to ten breast cancer patients that need extra help to have a special Christmas. One of the first recipients used some of the funds to pay bills and the rest to buy some holiday presents for her two children for whom she could not have gotten anything. Shortly after Christmas, we received a thank you telling us this and it made a lot of us cry, particularly when we found out a couple of weeks later she passed away." –Rick

Instructions:

1. Discover a service or product you can create for the purpose of memorializing your wife. Feel free to conduct the activity on your own or with a group that also shares your desire for memorializing your wife's memory.

2. Coordinate the materials and the core group of supporters and set out to make an initial quantity of product. If it is a service such as providing handyman skills, maybe the product can be to offer advice on much needed home repairs or actually perform simple repairs for the elderly free of labor charges.

3. Sell your product or services at work or through word of mouth. Maybe a restaurant or bar will help promote you. Ask clergy, your local support groups (hospice, clinics, associations) and fellow co-workers for ideas on how to get them distributed to the public. You will be amazed at how many options you will ponder.

4. You may choose to collect money to continue to reinvest and do more as an ongoing social club type group or decide that a specific financial goal will be the end of the effort.

Journaling follow-up:

1. What is a skill or activity I am committed to pursue which will fill my idle time by assisting others?

2. What were some feelings I experienced while I was serving others, perhaps some with needs greater than mine?

3. How was this activity meaningful to my wife and how did it provide an increased sense of connection to her and honor her memory?

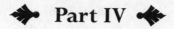

Part IV

Loving Again

"To fear love is to fear life,
and those who fear life are already three parts dead."
Bertrand Russell

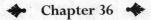

Chapter 36

Share
Lessons Learned

When we experience the loss of a spouse, we quickly learn how ignorant we were about death and the dying process and how much we need the help of others to pull through it. This is particularly true in the case of a long-term illness such as cancer because having fore-knowledge of death affords us the opportunity to lean on others and pre-pare as best we can. However, when the cause of death is sudden and pre-ventable such as a workplace fatality or a drunken driving accident, accepting death can be more difficult and support from others becomes even more necessary. In these cases, there was no time to prepare and acclimate oneself to the eventuality that grief was imminent.

Regardless of the cause of death, during the experience we learn a spectrum of knowledge that we never dreamt we would. Perhaps we learn medical terminology and treatment protocols; maybe we discover gaps in laws that we thought were in place to protect us. We quickly dis-covered that we needed to learn about a whole new world if we stand a chance of surviving this hardship. People along the way have helped us, but ultimately, we have to piece together our own plan for all this infor-mation to make sense, give us direction and have peace of mind we are doing the best thing for us and our family's future.

***

This Is How I'd Do It

Sharing lessons learned with others is a strong theme with those who experience the loss of a spouse through an extended life-ending situation. Men and women caregivers have struggled equally with a strong sense of helplessness as they attempted to offer physical and emotional assistance during their loved one's life ending process. After their loved one's death, the opportunity to assist others in need provides a well deserved sense of purpose once again.

Both genders experience a renewed sense of altruism as they see their effort of reaching out to others as one choice in life in which they have some element of control. The act of sharing knowledge, whether by offering specific advice as another person journeys through the health care system, or by simply providing a listening ear or words of encouragement, will provide a feeling of *I can make a difference and provide a ray of hope for another person.*

***

This activity is dedicated to using this newfound knowledge for the benefit of others. You do not want others to walk the same path that you have just traveled. Your help and shared information can make all the difference for someone. Sharing your knowledge can make another's loss much more tolerable, and you will undoubtedly feel a sense of accomplishment knowing that you are improving his situation. Helping others avoid the pitfalls you endured will turn part of your grief into a positive experience.

To more clearly understand how you can help another, ask yourself how many questions you had during your struggle and how difficult it seemed to get a quality answer quickly. How many decisions did you feel that you needed more time to make? What critical knowledge of yours would you share with another person if you knew he was walking the same path you were on just a short time ago? What would have been different for you if a person with the knowledge you now have was at your side during your battle? I would have been more at ease knowing valuable information was flowing my way that might have made problems more manageable for me and my sons.

While the battle for your wife's life may have been lost, the war for survival still rages for others on numerous fronts. Many of these people are operating on thin hope not unlike the hope that fed your desire to defeat your wife's illness and death. Whether you have lost your wife to a fatal illness or a sudden death, you can be this coach to others. Just by telling your story to someone in mourning, you can give them a new perspective on their situation that they may not have come up with themselves. For example, in the event of a fatality due to an auto accident, maybe sharing the knowledge you learned about the law from a similar situation or providing a legal resource may help another person feel that someone is watching out for them. Anyone who has lost a wife for any reason can be a comfort to those who are grieving, just as you had needs for supportive others when your loss first affected you.

***

"I don't give specific instructions to people and tell them what to do, but if they ask me, I give them all the information they are willing to take from me. You learn a lot when you spend five and a half years fighting cancer. It helps me a lot to be able to share this knowledge that has gotten me through the tough times." –Rick

***

You can grow in ways you never thought possible by sharing time with those who may be following the road you just traveled. Within a few months of losing Terri to breast cancer, I learned that a co-worker's wife was diagnosed with the same disease. I invited him to lunch, because I knew from my personal experience how the uncertainty of this disease can become an overriding cause of fear and hopelessness in one's mind. I had no idea what I was going to say, do or feel, but I knew I had to at least listen and provide a shoulder to lean on even if it was only for an hour at lunch. In that time, I learned his wife's situation was grim, but I did offer him a few notes of encouragement and particularly reminded him to talk about all the desires and wishes she had for him and their children. I made it a point to tell him that no matter how hard it might be to converse about such deep and meaningful topics, he would cherish those discussions no matter which way her condition would turn. I told him it would help to ease her concerns for the future as well as his own, because they would both know what they truly wanted for each other. He left that lunch knowing it was the loving thing to do. I experienced such a tremendous feeling of reward when I helped that man by talking with him for an hour. I am certain he followed up on it and held those conversations of love with his wife.

Another example illustrates the importance of sharing your learning with others. In our battle with breast cancer, there were many instances where Terri and I felt we were inventing our plan as time elapsed. This by no means implies we weren't prepared for tests or doctor appointments and the like. Just the opposite was true. We were so prepared that often-times we were asking questions of people and got reactions similar to "no one ever asked us that before." Our oncologist often commented that he wished all of his patients took as active an approach to beating their cancer as we had shown. However, even the most tenacious person will want to give up and your support may be all that she needs to continue.

After being denied insurance coverage for a chemotherapy that cost $10,500 per month, I managed during an election year to gain a guber-natorial candidate's influence on the insurance company. I simply asked the right person to help us and she did. After a few select phone calls, the insurance company not only paid for the drug from that point forward, but also retroactively for the funds we personally took out of a retirement investment. This experience is a favorite I use to convince someone who is battling a difficult issue that seems insurmountable. I tell them to never believe the first six "NOs" you get. Keep asking until you get a "YES". To this day, I get responses from people in the medical profession who sim-ply cannot believe I was able to pull this feat off. This is not to blow my own horn on how I went the extra mile for Terri, but a testament to the reason to share one's experiences with others for their benefit and future successes when they believe their plan is falling apart.

You might doubt the effect you can have on someone else's situation. Don't sell yourself short. Maybe the benefit you could give is just minimizing his pain through a comforting conversation you can share with him. You might be able to contribute other resources that can help his experience be a more positive one. That resource could be financial, emotional support, organizational management or information sharing. For example, your experience in dealing with insurance companies or your political connections can help another punch through a difficult issue. It may be as simple as making a phone call or two for someone who is overwhelmed by his situation or simply offering advice based on your personal experience.

We may doubt our ability to contribute as individuals, but we have so many diverse skills and so much knowledge with which we can help those in need. However, you need to choose to help, whether your assistance reaches out to one person or it touches many lives. Such simple acts can change the world for another person—and that makes all the difference.

Instructions:

1. Seek out a charity, church or other organization and ask about helping a specific family in need similar to the path you experienced. Describe how your skills and the knowledge you learned could be helpful to this family. Due to privacy reasons, the organization may require that they make the first contact and offer of help to the family and then you will be contacted. Once contact is made, discuss how you can best help.

2. Ask family, friends and co-workers if they know of anyone who may be experiencing a difficult time with grieving. You might want to do something very simple for them such as loaning your reading materials, DVDs, audio CDs or even just a contact list of people you feel can help the grieving person through his rough spot. You may want to leave the offer open and let the person decide when to call.

3. Contact a family that experienced a death and make your offer of help by combining this task with that of chapter 40, "Send Your Sympathies." In your sympathy card, include your offer to help and a means to contact you.

Journaling follow-up:

1. What new knowledge have I acquired that I can share with others in an effort to make their paths more tolerable to travel?

2. How did my effort in sharing this knowledge help turn my grief into a positive experience?

3. How would the path with my wife have been different if we had been given advice from a person with the knowledge I have now?

Chapter 37

Clothe Others

The vast majority of people judge one another on appearances long before they get to know the true person behind the clothing, hairstyles or hygiene. The impression is further made with verbal speech and physical body language. We have even felt it ourselves whether we care to admit it or not. Everyone at one time or another has experienced the embarrassment of being poorly dressed when someone stopped by for an unannounced visit, or felt the uneasiness of being underdressed at a social function.

The result was a sense of being slightly uncomfortable, an outcast of sorts. We just didn't feel like we fit in or worse yet, felt undeserving to be in attendance. When you cannot afford good quality clothing when an important event like a job interview presents itself, the feeling is even worse. Even though you may be well qualified for the position, you just don't shine through because something as simple as poor clothing stands in the way.

After giving some of your wife's possessions to family and friends, you may find there are still many items that hang in her closet or lie in her drawers. The donation of your wife's clothing to a YMCA / YWCA or similar charity utilizes what she has left behind for the benefit of needy individuals. Giving your wife's wardrobe to charities that focus on providing clothing for job interviews can be a great way to give to others after her death. These second chance closets clothe people in professional attire when the original store price would have been prohibitive for them. Of course, there are everyday items that also deserve consideration for donation to charitable organizations. All clothing and everyday items donated to local charities help them create jobs and raise funds through the sale of such gifted belongings.

***

I'll Do What I Want

Tom reveals, "Throughout my twenty plus years in counseling men and women in grief after the death of their spouses, the issue of when and how to part with their loved ones' belongings has been a sensitive topic for debate. There is no evidence to suggest a right or wrong way to disburse one's spouse's clothing. In my experience, there are also no distinct gender differences in the timing or method of parting with the deceased's clothes."

The act of donating one's clothing to a worthy cause such as a local charity will provide a strong sense of altruism, helping others in need while maintaining yet one more emotional connection with the deceased. In the end, do what feels right for you. Don't let someone try to convince you that clearing out your late wife's closet will get you over your grief any sooner.

***

Parting with the effects of the deceased is often a difficult task. Clothing can be particularly difficult because it not only characterizes the person, but it was physically touching your dear one's body every day. As time goes on, this uneasiness towards giving away her clothing may pass. It might also be easier to give these items to family members.

Others, however, can't wait to get rid of the visual and tactile reminder of having a closet full of their wives' clothes. Walking into a closet every day and seeing them is a constant visual reminder that the clothes are not moving into and out of the closet—a sign that the loved one is truly gone from the Earth. Nevertheless, please keep in mind that the longer the clothes sit and become dated, the less use they are to anybody.

***

"I had the family come in and take what they wanted, and what was left I gave to a local charity. Looking at her clothes wasn't going to help me or do me any good." –Jerry B.

***

Terri was a teacher and had a significant wardrobe of professional clothing, and because she often gave my son's winter coats to students who needed them, I knew what to do to honor her memory. It was a very easy decision to donate her clothes to help lift the spirit of other human beings. The ecstatic reaction I received from those volunteers was so genuine; it gave me a true sense of good will for my fellow man. I knew those clothes were going to help a number of people and it made me feel great!

Do your wife the honor of donating her clothes to a charity. Women's shelters especially welcome career clothing, as their clients need it since they may have left an abusive home without packing their belongings. As Mark Twain once said, "Clothes make the man." Help someone feel more like a whole person and lift his or her esteem by providing them the opportunity to feel dressed for success.

Instructions:

1. Call your local YMCA/YWCA, church, Salvation Army or Goodwill and ask about clothing banks for job interviews or other purposes.
2. Collect the clothing that your deceased wife used in the workplace for donation. You don't need to give everything away in one transaction. Remember to give things to friends and family and to save several items for other projects in this book.
3. You may wish to donate other items that will not be used such as unopened cosmetics and similar non-symbolic items.

Journaling follow-up:

1. Which of my wife's clothes am I comfortable donating to a needy organization or charity and to which charity?
2. What has helped me to become able to emotionally part with my wife's clothing?
3. How does the act of donating my wife's clothing to charity help to honor her?

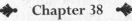

Chapter 38

Bestow
a Seat

After the death of a wife, widowers often feel a shift in their need to offer assistance to others. This outcome becomes almost a radical shift in their sense of purpose and they speak of this often as one of their major life changes. Men typically have a larger sense of being needed by others than women report. Previously focused on providing primarily for a wife and family, men fulfill this need now by replacing the wife's and immediate family's needs with needs of others.

I will never forget the value of a good seat and the feeling we had when Terri and I were offered a prime seat that we definitely did not deserve. A long time ago, the three of us, my eldest son, Terri who was pregnant, and I, were visiting Disney World. For some reason, our son would not sit in the rental strollers, yet complained incessantly about the walking. This went on for over two days at the park. Upon entrance to the park on the third day, a Disney employee took one look at Terri's condition and quickly offered her a wheelchair as we stood in line to rent a stroller to try again. After all, we weren't about to let a four-year-old crack us at his game! The instant the wheelchair came out from the back, lo and behold, our son wanted a ride in it! We thought, *Hey problem solved!* All day long the two took turns riding in the wheelchair that dad pushed along. Later that night, as we were racing to get in line for a live performance of the very popular *Beauty & the Beast* stage show, we turned the final corner of the street only to see a line that seemed miles long to get into the show. We exclaimed an apparent heavy sigh in unison because it was obvious to us we were much too late to even get into the show.

Then suddenly, and without warning, a Disney employee noticed us and immediately grabbed the wheelchair from my hands and said, "Right this way, sir. Wheelchairs need not wait in the line!" I was astounded as he raced Terri and my son through the gate and down the main aisle towards the stage. I couldn't utter a word of correction to his assumption of our need. We HAD NO NEED! But he ended his route at the front row center of the stage where several other wheelchairs and their owners were positioned. Here we were, sitting in prime seats of a "must see" show for which moments earlier we were thinking we wouldn't get into the theater! I tried to explain to the Disney usher we didn't need this seat and how we came to have the wheelchair, but he would not hear of it, only saying, "Enjoy the show"! The kindness of the Disney staff stuck in our memories as a favorite pregnancy story told many times long after that day!

***

"Donna had spent much of her working career at a local bank as a personal banker where she thoroughly enjoyed helping people secure finances for making their dreams come true. Her personal interest in people was the direct cause for why she often topped all other bankers in monthly business measures for loan performance. I wanted to somehow pay tribute to her memory so that others would never forget how she made a point to be focused on the people first. I was told by the bank manager that a bench with a plaque honoring her work couldn't be allowed at the bank due to it possibly starting precedence for other such memorials for which they had no room. But, I knew I still had a shot with the city. They gladly accepted my offer to donate a bench because they were in the process of replacing ones in the city's Japanese garden. What really made this especially fitting was that Donna and I spent the first two years of our marriage in Japan. It's strange how events play out in life, but I think all things happen for a reason. The garden is a very fitting place for her bench where it will last for a very long time offering assistance to others who may need a place to rest. The plaque was cast in bronze and is mounted on a concrete bench so I know countless people will use the bench and see the plaque for many years and come to know that she especially touched someone's life." —Larry

***

Offering a seat to someone is a great way to demonstrate to *yourself* that you can be a servant to others and receive intrinsic satisfaction versus a physical sense of satisfaction by using the seat for yourself. It is probably the simplest act of kindness one can show for another and without cost. The feeling of servitude is so significant from such a small deed that you can't help but feel good inside when you do it. Here are a few ideas for giving up a seat!

- Next time you are seated and in a public location where others are in need of a seat, offer yours to another. Notice their reaction. Some will refuse the offer because they have not had the experience of being offered such a small but meaningful act of kindness. Insist on them taking it.

- Give a lasting seat to more than one person by calling up your local park system. Offer to pay for and have a park bench installed somewhere along a walking trail or similar location where it will be used. Pick a scenic spot where the users will be inclined to use it. Good candidates for benches are historical living museums where many people will be walking around. Ask if a small plaque can be added to the bench to indicate that your deceased wife is being memorialized with this bench.

- Donate funds for your church or place of worship where pews or other furniture may be needed. Your church or place of worship may even point you to another facility such as a homeless shelter or other charity where furniture may be needed.

- Donate a chair or sofa your wife once used to Goodwill for another family to benefit from it.
- Call your local school system or college and ask if they have a means to memorialize your wife with a seat in an auditorium or football bleacher.
- If you do not have the abilities or resources to construct a bench but want to memorialize your wife in a major construction project, look for projects where benches, auditorium chairs and even cafeteria and soup kitchen seats can be memorialized. Churches often have such memorial projects available. Maybe your wife's favorite sports team is building a new stadium and is asking for donations in return for an inscribed plaque on their supporter's wall. Even after the construction is completed, there are typically still seats available for individualizing. Also, your local chamber of commerce can help you find such projects.

There are so many ways you can honor the memory of your wife through the simple act of providing someone a seat. Don't be afraid to call your friends who may have some woodworking skills or be involved in a local garden society that could help you realize this dream. This one gift will be appreciated by many people over the years, so enjoy completing it and know that it will have a lasting impact on others who will be reminded of your wife's contribution.

Instructions:

1. Pick one of the ideas mentioned or create one of your own that can memorialize your wife by creating a place of relaxation or enjoyment for another. Be sure to have her name on a plaque or similar designation in the location so that others know your kindness to the needs of others.

Journaling follow-up:

1. How and where have I created a memorial seat symbolizing my wife's kindness to others?
2. How did I feel during and after performing this act, both in regards to my own reaction in addition to the recipient's reaction to the act?
3. How has my wife's influence in living a life of kindness heightened my desire to live a similar life, as a means of carrying out her legacy?

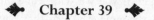

Chapter 39

Gain a
New Perspective

It is understandable if a feeling of a hopeless future pervades a grieving person's thinking. The massive change and emotional pain that occurs with a loved one's death seems unbearable. How can we expect that we will ever be able to view our own sorrows as an experience which will bring strength, understanding and a sense of joy?

The answer lies in committing yourself to sharing with others, your grief and how it has changed your view of life. This chapter asks you to grieve openly to others the hardships you have felt in great detail. Discussing the details of your pains will illustrate not only what you have endured, but also how those feelings radically changed your viewpoint on life priorities and sense of purpose. By doing so, you are laying it out in the open for anyone to feel your sense of loss and in effect challenging them to see their world in a different light. Such an in-depth discussion will cause them a moment of self-reflection that may be incredibly beneficial to them. They may be taking many aspects of their lives for granted, and a brief conversation with you may influence their viewpoint and affect lasting change.

You might also be thinking that sharing your grief with others in such detail will not get you into a joyous mindset. This might be true in the immediate timeframe. However, we can choose to turn grief into something positive. By openly sharing our emotional pains and how they influence our life choices with others, then maybe we will heal a bit faster with this intrinsic reward and help others recognize the joys they have in their lives.

***

A Wrong Turn

Over one hundred years ago, during the Victorian era, grieving was considered a natural and acceptable part of the culture. Death and grief were popular subjects for music and literature. It was commonplace to see a person in mourning wearing black clothing, a black arm band or a black veil. The home of a bereaved family would have a black wreath on the front door announcing publicly that this was a home of sorrow. Bereavement was conspicuous, and there were very specific societal customs designed to support people during the mourning process.

How different it is now over one hundred years later! We have done a cultural 180 degree turn. Grief and mourning have suddenly become a closeted issue. In many circles it is not considered polite nor in good taste to forthrightly mention the sadness caused by death. Well-mannered bereaved people (especially men) are expected to keep their pain private and silenced.

Men and women in grief both need to declare their freedom from the restraints placed on them by a frightened society. Society must let men and women kindly, but firmly, declare their rights to feel and express their pain in ways that are healthy and open. With that right, of course, comes the responsibility to do no harm to others. With kindness and a do-no-harm attitude, one can take a firm stand and feel no remorse for doing so just because society isn't fully accepting of the bereaved. People must feel free to speak out about their losses, verbalize their emotions, solicit and expect help and support and make no apologies for their condition. Ultimately, you as a person in grief should never feel silenced by the ignorance of those who have not walked in your sandals. Speak out and enlighten another to your world of grief—it's your right.

***

Shortly before Terri's death, I was engaged in a conversation with a professional health care provider whom I know very well. He was going on and on, complaining about his relationship with his wife and sons who didn't seem to care about his housekeeping standards. He mentioned as an example that no one in his household thought about rinsing out ice cream dishes after their use before placing them in the dishwasher. He went on to complain that unless he did it, it would not get done and the unsightly dried-on ice cream dishes would remain in the sink. After a while of listening to his complaints, I couldn't help but mention to him that if this was all he had to complain about in his world, he was living pretty damned good. I asked him to trade places with me—to look at what I was dealing with and to reassess his situation. I told him I would gladly take on his stress in place of mine. He quickly realized how insignificant his complaints seemed to me and was embarrassed.

While it didn't necessarily make me instantly feel better at the time, I now look upon that moment from a new vantage point. I learned that sometimes you just have to be blunt with people and tell them to appreciate what they have in life because others have far less. My perspective years earlier might have been the same as my friend's, but it now has definitely changed to focus on the more important things in life. This new attitude is just one example of a "joy". In fact, I would go a step further and say I feel actually blessed by having gained this refreshed outlook. Now, I have increased sensitivity to other people's needs. One of the most important values I learned from losing Terri is that I now strive to have compassion for people when they need it the most and good judgment to motivate people in the right direction when they are being self-centered.

Because I have learned so much from Terri's death, I cannot help but become engaged with anyone who will discuss the lessons I have learned by this life changing experience. This is not because I am still fixated on grieving her death, but because I am truly interested in challenging others to possibly re-evaluate their attitudes towards life. Recovering from the loss of my wife has tuned me in to life's important matters and thus has made it easy for me to discern others' needs. I find that the more I openly talk about what her death has meant to my life, it becomes increasingly easy to talk about the new perspective that I now hold dear.

There are many opportunities that you can take advantage of to help others gain a fresh perspective of life's true priorities and purpose. Some ideas that you may want to consider include the following:

- **Sharpen a friend's perspective on how to share love:** Illustrate the idea that love is all there is. With this simple message, challenge your listener to remove all doubt the next time they indicate love to another person.

- **Write to someone with whom you can empathize:** Write a letter to a friend who may need some encouragement on a tough issue. Consider his or her situation and think about an experience you had that was similar and how you got support to overcome your hardship. Write about your experience in a way that clearly illustrates how you can feel the person's pain but that he or she will pull through it because you are at his or her side offering your experienced assistance. By describing your innermost feelings of uncertainty and helplessness, the other person will see that he or she can rely on you for support.

- **Challenge someone to be kind:** Make a small token that you can carry around with you that has these words written on it, "I choose to be kind versus being right." The token can be a simple laminated piece of tag-board, a metal machine washer or a stone from a garden with the words written on it with a permanent marker. Next time you engage in a debate with someone over a small issue, reach for that token in your pocket and change your tone to be kind. You may want to forgo your position and allow the decision to go the other person's way. After doing so, hand the person the token and ask him or her to keep it until needed. This idea will work wonders as the token is passed between family members or co-workers several times. Take notice how changing your position from being right to being kind had significance on your sense of happiness and the sense it left the other person. Try to do this all the time and you will see that there are many insignificant issues that people are willing to fight over because of their myopic perspectives.

- **Challenge your community to squabble less:** Write a guest column in your local paper's public opinion page or a letter to you city council members. Pick a topic where you believe the community may benefit from your perspective. By challenging your community to rise above squabbling on an insignificant issue, you might just spark the decision of one reader who may be the influential vote on the city council.

***

"After my experience in losing Barb, I had several opportunities to share my feelings with people very close to me about choices they were making in their lives. Losing your wife can give you a lot of wisdom that others may never discover. You can tell them your story, give them the perspective you have, but in the end, it's their choice." –Mike

***

Whether the new perspective you wish to impart on others is about sharing love, writing letters to enlighten or pointing out the difference of righteousness versus kindness, your wife's death can personalize a key issue for others to take notice. They can now connect or relate better to the problem because they see how the problem directly affected someone they personally know or someone in their community. When people take notice and a problem becomes personalized for them, they will typically find it hard not to take action. So use this opportunity to share your new viewpoints with others on a grander scale than ever imagined, and you will see your joys start to emerge from the sadness of losing your wife.

Instructions:

1. Choose one or more of the ideas mentioned or create something else that communicates publicly what this wonderful person meant to you and what new perspectives could be learned from her death.

Journaling follow-up:

1. What opportunities have I taken to share my grief with others and how has it changed my view of life?
2. How has my experience of sharing my grief impacted my life priorities and sense of purpose?
3. How has enduring my experiences in losing my wife specifically helped others learn from me?

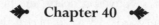

Chapter 40

Send Your Sympathies

Every day, people all around us, including family, friends, co-workers and unknown people in our community, lose loved ones. Death is a natural part of life, as is birth. Unfortunately, Western culture treats death and the grieving process in a much more reserved and private manner than other cultures of the world. We have very few conversations about death, even with the closest members of our families. We are reluctant to share our beliefs regarding the process of dying, the afterlife, grieving or the celebration of one's life. We are therefore not as prepared as we could be when death strikes close to us. This is true even in situations of immanent loss.

A man who has previously endured the grieving process of losing a wife can have a considerable consoling effect to one who is mourning the loss of his wife. Such experienced people are typically willing to share their deepest feelings about death and dying to those who are suffering, for they easily recall their own experiences and can relate to the grieved. You are in a unique position to console others, because you have suffered as well, so share it with someone for both of you to benefit.

I am personally grateful for having discussions soon after Terri passed away with three people who also lost family members. Two had lost daughters in childhood and the third also lost his wife to cancer. Each of them had a unique perspective on death, the purpose of it and how it affected their lives afterwards. I was surprised that while they had very comforting thoughts to share with me, they each gave me and my family something unique to think about. Their comments seemed to be what I exactly needed to hear in that moment. I know that their reaching out to me gave me a sense of comfort that helped to close my wound just a little bit more.

I also received so many wonderful cards and letters informing me what type of person Terri was and how people's thoughts were with me and my sons. There was an outpouring of donations, which I eventually gave to a local breast cancer charity group that provides support for women suffering from the disease. I was overwhelmed by the thought of sending a meaningful thank you card to all of these caring people and to make it a genuine response to their thoughtful gestures, but in some way, I never grew tired of writing them and each card I wrote meant more and more to me and my healing process. I eventually realized that there were other people to whom I needed to say "thank you" who were not expecting this gratitude. For example, I sent a card to Terri's oncologist who was just doing his job, but I needed to let him know, in a formal and private way, that his efforts didn't fail us and that his presence made our difficult road all the more bearable.

There are many ways you can heal your feelings of loss and see a brighter tomorrow if you help others realize that they are not alone. Read your newspaper or go online to find the obituaries of your community. As you read through the notices, try to identify someone with whom you can have some spiritual or meaningful connection. The person who has died may have suffered from the same disease as your wife, had the same career or may have served in the same armed forces as your wife or you. To this day, long after Terri's death from breast cancer, I empathize when I read of another woman who leaves behind young children. Because of this, I make it a point to reach out to those affected by this terrible disease. Whatever the method, pick someone with whom you have some small connection.

After you note the obituary on someone who has passed on, think of the family she left behind. She might have had a husband, children and other relatives she must have loved. Stop for a moment and say a prayer or hold a meditative thought about the subject's spirit and the people she loved. Surely, you can feel their grief as you have felt your loss. Wish upon all of them the peace and comfort they will need to get through their loss. Request that their loss be healed in the best and most rewarding way it can.

Follow up on your thoughts and send them a simple sympathy card with a brief message explaining that your thoughts are with them. You might want to explain the connection you feel to them if you wish. The simple act of receiving a card from a perfect stranger will be rewarding in itself. By bestowing love and feelings of comfort on another individual, you can receive these same thoughts indirectly for yourself. You will be lighting up a fire of love within your own heart that will help you heal as well.

***

Express Sympathy Sensitively

Jim from Tom's "Understanding Grief" group reported attending six funerals since his wife's death six months ago. Jim felt the strong, emotional connection between himself and the other bereaved that is only possible from their feelings of walking this road of grief together. Jim experienced a sincere sense of compassion, as he was able to comfort others in grief.

Often we ask, "What should I say in a sympathy card?" Here are some simple phrases that may help you:

- I want to help you share your burden. Would it be helpful if I were to…? (It is important to make a specific offer here because often a person grieving won't be capable of putting a to-do list together for people.)
- You are in my thoughts.
- Our thoughts and prayers are with you.
- We are thinking of you.

- We are deeply sorry to hear about the death of "name of deceased."
- Remember that we love and care about you.
- With loving memories of "name of deceased."
- Our hearts go out to you in your time of sorrow.
- "Name of deceased" will remain in our hearts forever.
- We pray the love of God enfolds you during your journey through grief.
- Please accept our most heartfelt sympathies for your loss…our thoughts are with you and your family during this time.
- May your heart and soul find peace and comfort.

The following are phrases that may not be appropriate to say:
- You're still young, you can always remarry.
- He/she led a full life.
- Death was a blessing.
- Perhaps it was his or her time.
- You will get over this in time.
- I understand how you feel. (While you could very well share similar situations, each person grieves differently.)
- Call me when you need anything. (A person or family that is grieving need to be able to say "yes" or "no" to an offer of help or assistance. It might be too taxing at this time for some to have to think of things for others to do, but they may keep in touch.)

***

"People may find that after losing a spouse that it may be more difficult to attend another person's funeral services. After my experience of losing Barb, I don't miss a funeral. Recently I went to a funeral of a family acquaintance of which I hadn't seen in twenty-five years. I walked into the service and noticed people looking at me kind of funny, clearly wondering who the heck I was. Once I started talking to the bereaved they couldn't believe it was me. They were glad to see me and I was glad to be there for them. So making a point to reach out to those in need is important to me. They were all there for me." –Mike

***

Instructions:

1. Find a person through the local obituaries who has some connection to you or your wife.
2. Hold a prayer or meditative thought in your mind for reaching out to comfort the person's loved ones left behind.
3. Carry the obituary throughout the day and send a thought about them each time you make contact with the clipping. Make your thought as simple as you wish, focusing on the comfort you wish to bestow onto them.
4. Go online and add the person's name to a prayer ring (see chapter 5, "Seek the Prayer Connection") or add it to one at your congregation.
5. Send a sympathy card to the immediate family, indicating what you did and that even though you are a perfect stranger, you prayed for the family's comfort and feel their sense of loss as well. You might mention if their loved one shared the same illness as your wife if that is the case.

Journaling follow-up:

1. Who is one person I feel I can reach out to as a means of providing sympathy and support?
2. In what ways have my past and more recent experiences with my wife prepared me to be a valuable source of support to others dealing with grief?
3. How has the value of the support I received influenced my willingness to offer sympathy to another?

Chapter 41

Appreciate
Love and
Marriage

After the death of a wife, the impact of being without a companion is felt in almost everything a widower does. The loss of a partner for intimate conversation or just to share the day's events impacts one at the very core of the pain of grief. The feeling of isolation of being permanently cut off from the only one who understood weighs heavily on the bereaved, and there is neither a quick fix nor a perceived and possible long-term solution on the horizon. The sound of silence can be deafening, but loss of interaction through conversation only explains a portion of the feelings of emptiness that widowers report. The missing physical connections of a hug, kiss, playful love tap and sexual intimacy contributes significantly to feelings of despair.

Widowers feel this boundless depression so painfully that many strive to repair this aspect of their new lives almost immediately. They look to fill the need for adult companionship by quickly immersing themselves in new relationships with hopes that others can understand them as they had enjoyed previously with their deceased wives. Some may not act so quickly as they may become frozen, wondering if new relationships would be approved of by their deceased spouses. A wife who was able to share her thoughts that her husband should find new companionship with the widower prior to death may be all the license a man needs to feel enabled to pursue a new relationship. Others, however, may be conflicted because no such clarity on the issue was ever obtained.

***

Finding Love Again

Re-socialization is essential to reorganizing your life. Developing romantic relationships is something different. If this happens too soon, adequate adjustment to the loss of a spouse may not occur. It is very difficult to make the necessary separation from a spouse and develop close romantic ties to another person at the same time. One participant from a recent grief group remarried two months after his wife's death then divorced shortly after the marriage. This happened largely because he never allowed himself time to grieve for his first wife.

Factors that often contribute to a desire to remarry include perception of loneliness, unhappiness, depression, sadness and the need of a mother for young children. Widowers perceived the need for friendship, companionship, adult interaction and the need for the love of a woman.

***

"My biggest struggle was being home alone at night. All day long, I would keep busy, golfing, running errands, etc., but ultimately I had to go home and there was nobody there. So I really appreciate the time I spend with my girlfriend. My daughters are still getting use to it and that's understandable to some degree, but my friends are really supportive of me having a companion. I can't spend all of my time with my children's families. They have their own lives to live. I'm not looking to replace Marge, because she always will be irreplaceable to me. Marge telling me not to sit and mourn her after she was gone was a big help for me to get comfortable with having my girlfriend." –Joe

***

I was fortunate to have "discussed" this tough issue with Terri through the journaling we traded. I needed to know what she thought would be best for me and my sons. In my journal, I expressed to her that someday when my sons had families of their own, they should not be saddled with the guilt of having to constantly keep me entertained. Terri and I had retirement goals and she didn't want to see me have to give those up just because I was single. Goals such as traveling are hard to realize, even harder to enjoy if you have no one with whom to share the experience. Terri knew my social nature and therefore knew that my happiness would best be served if someone was with me to share in the experiences of life. Her answer that she would "send someone to me" was all that I needed to hear. Her approval to open my heart to another is comforting to me. I have explained my dating to my sons by ensuring they understand:

1. **I am not searching for a replacement for their mother.** No one can replace her as they will only have one mother. We are a team of three and doing just fine.

2. **Just as I love them equally, they still are two individuals.** Just as I loved their mother, there can be another woman for me who can bring back a relationship of happiness into my life. My love for their mother will always be different than the love I could ever have for another. Different isn't anything less, it's just not the same.

3. **I am not on any timeline.** And if it never happens, I still feel blessed by having spent twenty years with Terri while some people may never experience such happiness.

Whether or not you have clarity as to what your wife may have desired for you, ultimately your personal lifestyle that leads you to happiness in the long term is what will count for your total sense of well being.

***

"I think if one has children, particularly young children, there should be high concern for their thoughts and feelings about reconnecting with another woman. It is especially important that they understand you do not love your late wife any less by dating again. You need to take the time to ensure they understand that life does deal families bad hands and as hard as it is, you have to move on." –Mark

***

"I took my marriage vows seriously and I think the phrase 'until death do us part' makes it clear that the life I did have with Barb is now in the past and it gives me a sense of permission that I can move on. You never forget the past—good times or bad—but you can move on for the future. If you have any doubts about re-marrying, don't do it. And if they can't cook, definitely don't do it!" —Mike (who is now remarried)

***

Dating is the first stepping-stone for crossing the waters towards the life of a new relationship. Some widowers experience a sense of fear in having been out of circulation for so long. I have referred to this as the "knocking-the-rust-off" phase. My earlier dates with women seemed a bit awkward and forced, but it comes back to you. I think trying to establish communication with a woman actually is easier now than in the early days as a teenager. Just think of all the facets you polished over the years of your life and you'll have plenty of subject material to talk about.

How can a guy years removed from the dating scene get back into circulation? Three simple ways: ask friends to help, get involved in social groups and join a dating service. The first way is probably the easiest to do, but may not lead you to the best results. My friends have been more than helpful giving me leads that they thought would be good for me. However, needless to say, even a close friend's opinions as to who might be a great match for me and my sons can be quite far from the mark.

Social groups in which you are a member can be a great way to meet others. You will be surprised at the number of people who are out there but have not been noticed by you because, quite frankly, you just weren't in the game. If you are not involved in hobby clubs or charitable organizations, join one or two. Soon you will find options from which to choose instead of those from a matchmaker friend.

Probably the easiest way to meet people is to use a dating service. This includes both online and local dating firms. The sheer volume of people online and the vast number of dating services is almost a perfect analogy to the many fish in the sea. Such is the breadth and depth of Internet dating that several books have already been published for how to navigate those waters. Whether it is online or through a local dating service, the options are vast, and the key here is that you have control over whom you will meet.

I have purposefully left out the option of meeting people spontaneously such as at parties, bars or other public venues. Reason being is that if this method works for your style, you will not find it hard to use this approach in meeting people; however, it must be said that as a widower, you may find such a practice to be very inefficient with the limited time resources you have.

When you start to date, you may find yourself on the receiving end of some unexpected feedback from others. This can range from a "good for you" to "it's too early to be out there—give it a year." What others may say is exactly that—another person's opinion. As long as you follow a dating process that respects your family, children and the women you date, then you should feel positive about taking steps towards building future relationships. Some adult family members may feel very offended that you have started dating too soon, feeling that you have not given your grief sufficient time to heal. Again, explain that that you are not out to replace your deceased wife and that dating in no way diminishes the love you had for her.

***

"I have no desire at this time to date or seek someone. But, I do have concerns of what others would think and say if I were to start seeing someone. Donna and I had such a close marriage I cannot see myself sharing my life with someone else at this time. I think the following line makes my feelings clear—If we love deeply, we must suffer deeply; for the price of ecstatic joy is anguish. And so it was with us to the end." —Larry

***

"I did find someone through an online dating Web site. What am I going to do? I have kids and I'm not about to leave them at home and go sit in a bar to find someone. I think it's tough for my wife's family to see me dating. They need to understand that my dating in no way is a reflection on whether I loved Robin or not—I loved her as deeply as anyone could love a person. In a way, the love we did share is what I want to get back in my life with someone. I miss it." —Scott

***

There is no set schedule for grief healing. There is nothing magical about being alone for a year before venturing out towards new relationships. Everyone heals his grief on his own timetable, and sometimes just reaching out to another adult woman early on may be just a chance to have a companion to get away from the loneliness of a quiet house. Just because you spend time with a woman shortly after your wife's death doesn't mean she can't be a good friend.

In the early stages of dating anyone, keep in mind that initially you will want to be discrete and not feel the need to introduce every woman you meet to your children or in-laws. This is because you will find that it may take several dates spanning weeks to a few months to determine if you are even remotely compatible before subjecting children to a potentially revolving door of visitors. The last thing you need is for your children to become emotionally connected to someone whom you discover is not a suitable match for you in the long term, thereby creating more relationship harm than introducing someone who provides stabile feminine presence in their lives again. Then again, you may find a slow and steady pace is exactly what you need as well!

***

"Dating? Yes, I think there can be some real positives in doing it. I sometimes feel the need to talk to an adult and it's an outlet of sorts to have this kind of time with another who really can listen and converse with you. I think we are all meant to be with someone. I think my wife would wish it for me and the boys if the right gal would come along and provide some of that happiness again. Marriage? I'm not sure, maybe someday. Of course, I would really consider how my kids felt about her." —Ross

***

"Would I ever remarry? Right now I'd say no, but you never know what's going to happen!" —Jerry B. (age seventy-nine)

***

"I think I am resigned to stay by myself. We never had children so it was just me and her. I'm more of an introvert, so I'm thinking I'll find it much easier to stay by myself. Friends are trying to set me up, but it's my choice." —Rick

***

By the Numbers

For some, dating will eventually lead to thoughts regarding marriage. Since marriage is such an individualized subject, offering thoughts for or against it would be foolish. Instead, here are some interesting statistics on the subject that you may find helpful to contemplate:

- Common barriers to remarriage may include not wanting to or not having enough confidence to date again. There are often concerns regarding children from two separate families getting along in the new blended family. Those with dependent or disabled children find they are busy taking care of the children or that having children can be a deterrent to marriage prospects.

- Research on families in the United States is extensive, according to these studies. Sex differences and race differences exist in rates of remarriage. Compared with women, men remarry sooner and more often and generally marry women a few years younger. The more education and resources a man has, the more likely he is to remarry. Conversely, for women, having more education and resources and being older mean less likelihood of remarriage in general. Hispanic/Latino Americans remarry slightly less frequently and African-Americans remarry much less frequently than white, non-Hispanic Americans. It is not clear if these differences are due to cultural, religious or economic factors or some combination of the three.

- Being a parent lowers the likelihood of remarriage for women and men, but the effect of parenthood further lowers remarriage for women. With respect to parenthood in the remarriage, about half of women in remarriages give birth to at least one child and this usually happens within the first two years of the remarriage. Not surprising, as people age, the frequencies of remarrying and of re-divorcing decreases. However, in the twenty-first century, the number of later-life remarriages is expected to increase, as the baby boom generation will be living longer and healthier lives. When remarriage occurs after the death of a spouse, widowed men marry much sooner than widowed women, but all widowed people are much slower to remarry than divorced people.

The various attitudes enlisted of the interviewed illustrate that there is no consistent generalized attitude or belief system regarding remarriage. This has always been and will always be a very individual personal choice based on a variety of factors in an individual's life.

***

"I learned to do a lot of things when Marge was sick: cooking, laundry and cleaning the house. The funny thing is that I'd make someone a really good husband now!" —Joe

***

Instructions

1. It's your decision. Don't worry; be confident you'll make the right choice.

Journaling follow-up

1. What are my leading concerns about establishing a relationship with another woman?
2. What would I want to give to a new relationship? What would I expect to receive from a new relationship?
3. What have I learned in the relationship with my late wife that I can bring to others?

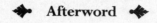 **Afterword**

I close by sharing with you a quotation from my cousin Constance Nelson, a teacher who lost her daughter at a very young age:

"You may feel that you are in a downpour now, but the sun will shine again. You may see it shining its light a little differently, but still it will shine again for you."

This book, I hope, will help make that sun shine as brightly as it can for you. To clearer skies...

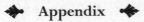

Appendix

Using the Bracelets

No doubt that you are familiar with the silicone bracelets many people are wearing these days to indicate their connection to a cause that has touched their lives. People wear bracelets as an act of support for a person that they care about, as a sign to others that the wearer is personally affected by this issue and finally to bring society's attention to the issue at large. Now it's your turn to wear a bracelet just for you.

Silicone wristbands for supporting you through your grief can be obtained at www.WidowersToolbox.com. They contain the message "A Time to Mourn… A Time to Heal…" The message is to remind you every day that while there will be dark moments in your new life without your spouse, you will experience healing moments as well.

The band can be worn daily to help you focus on honoring your wife throughout the activities in the chapters. Wearing the band will remind you that your upcoming task will create something good that will add to the positive side of this life-changing experience. When you are feeling a sudden sense of sadness, look to the band as a sign that you are clearing your path and getting your life back on track—all while honoring the life your wife shared with you.

You can use the band as a means to ignite conversation that will inspire you to educate your family and friends. If someone asks, "What is the meaning of the band you are wearing" you can tell them what you are doing to honor the memory of your wife. You can explain what you think it represents and why you feel the need to wear it. Dialog around such topics can spur helpful thoughts and build an understanding with others as to what is really helpful to your healing. Don't be surprised if they ask to participate with you in an activity for their own healing.

There are three ways in which the band can be used:

- Outside (Open Approach): Wear the band with the words shown on the exterior away from your wrist. With this method, it can be an opportunity to share with others your travel through grief.
- Inside (Semi-private Approach): Twist the band inside out so the words are on the inside—closest to your skin. This privatizes your mission and eliminates the need to discuss and explain your upcoming task to others. It stills serves to be a visual reminder of your journey, but does not blatantly advertise your intent to others.
- Concealed (Very Private Approach): Place the band in your pocket or on the inside of your wallet next to your paper currency. This will provide a means to see the band several times a day, yet keep it free from public view and shield you from fielding questions about its significance.

As you grieve your loss, you will find others who are traveling the same difficult path as yourself. Invite them to share in the tasks that you are performing in this book and they may also want bands of their own. Let them know how working with the book and wearing a band has helped you to heal. Then, after your journey through grief is completed, keep the band as a part of your journal. You may just find that it represents life's most difficult accomplishment.

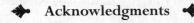 **Acknowledgments**

Thank you: These words simply cannot convey the truest sense of gratitude that I feel for those who helped make this book possible. However, at the risk of doing this in a way that is not nearly as profound as their assistance feels, I say simply "Thank you."

To God, I have eternal gratitude for giving me the love of my life and for improving my understanding of St. Paul's words in 1 Corinthians 13. I now understand what St. Paul meant far better than I ever conceived I would when I told Terri "I do".

I am indebted to all of the widowers who so graciously shared their deeply personal experiences so that readers can better understand that they are not alone and rebuilding lives again is truly possible. Larry Steuck, Mike Cizman, Scott, Ross Wiitanen, Rick Miller, Jerry Blindauer, Mark Knaus and Joe Roderick each brought his unique approach for getting his life back together for you the reader to see that there are many ways in which the rebuilding process can take place in one's life. Without these guys, this book simply would not have been possible.

I thank Megan Gregory, a talented writer whose knowledge and skills were instrumental in the initial stages of this project. Her assistance has been invaluable to me in exonerating my crimes against grammar and word usage and helping my story take a better form.

I am grateful for the test group participants, whose personal experiences due to the losses of their spouses afforded me the opportunity to learn more about people in grief and refine the initial concept of this book.

My appreciation to Maryann Karinch, who believed in this project from day one and took it from my passionate story of helping others to finding the best resources for making this book a reality. Maryann's willingness to take on risk with new writers to bring their writing to fruition is to be commended.

Unbounded thanks goes to Dr. Joan Dunphy and the staff at New Horizon Press. Joan's expertise and experience recognized the unmet needs of widowers in the marketplace, and her investment of resources has now made it possible for widowers to gain an alternate and useful form of grief help previously unavailable.

Lastly, I am indebted to all the people who played some role in encouragement, networking and belief in the project such that they gave personal time to its development along the way. Though I cannot include all who helped, I particularly thank Connie Worzala, Lisa De Sieno, Marcia Wiese, Kathy Leidig and the Fearless Freelancers writer's guild.

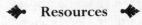

Chapter 1–Contact Other Professionals

In the first few pages of your local phone book under "Community Services", you will find listings for the Legal Aid Society, Lawyer Referral Service and the Bar Association. They provide an excellent service in the event you do not have a lawyer. Your phonebook will also have listings for your county court system that can point you to the right departments for filing your new legal status as a widower.

Social Security concerns can be addressed by visiting www.ssa.gov or by contacting them over the phone or in person at your nearest SSA office. You may find better success using the in-person route, but their phone number is listed in the "Government Listings" section of your phonebook.

The Veterans Administration or "VA" can also help you either online at www.va.gov or by contacting their department by locating them in the phonebook under the "Government Listings" section.

Chapter 5–Seek the Prayer Connection
Chapter 7–Get a Body/Mind/Spirit Tune-up
Chapter 8–Become Inspired

There are several popular authors and professionals in the area of enhancing your mindfulness and spiritual well-being. Here is a list of my favorites. I suggest you see for yourself what they might have to offer you:

Dyer, Wayne W. *Inspiration: Your Ultimate Calling*. New York: Hay House Inc., 2006.

The Web site www.griefshare.org is a great place to start learning more about grief, how others have dealt with it and a way to find a group where you can reach out to others who can lend an ear to help. The best part of this is that by being online, it can provide support at anytime—when you want to tap into it.

Chopra, Deepak. *The Book of Secrets: Unlocking the Hidden Dimensions of Your Life*. New York: Random House Inc., 2004.

Chapter 9–Learn to Meditate

The Brain Sync Company does an incredible job of offering a wide variety of topic specific meditation products. I have personally used Kelly Howell's meditation audio CDs with great success and highly recommend them for anyone wanting to learn more about the benefits that meditation can provide. "Brainwave Meditation" is a two-CD set which contains "Guided Meditation" and "Deep Meditation", which I highly recommend for people in grief. Other good choices include the "Faith" and "Healing Meditation" CDs. You can find them online at www.brainsync.com. Their contact information is: Brain Sync, P.O. Box 3120, Ashland, OR 97520 Phone: 800-444-SYNC (7962)

Chapter 10–Find Affirmations

The Pacific Institute has a long history of consulting with many Fortune 500 companies, sports teams and even governments of foreign countries to help clients become practitioners of their program to make lasting change in their environments. As a graduate of their program over twenty years ago, I found the techniques particularly helpful during my grief and I still practice them today. You can most easily find out more about them at their Web site www.pac-inst.com. Their contact information is: TPI International Headquarters, 1709 Harbor Ave, S.W., Seattle, WA 98126-6007 Phone: (206) 628-4800 or Phone: (800) 426-3660

Chapter 11–Make and Keep Friends

Aside from your own personal friends whom you could tap into for a helping hand why not try www.lotsahelpinghands.com. This Web site provides a quick portal to gaining the help that you might need even if you may not feel like asking. These people volunteer to help because they want to be there for you!

Chapter 29–Imagine the Other Side

Thought provoking reads that I recommend to open your mind to the possibilities of the other side include:

Brown, Silvia (with Harrison, Lindsay). *Life on the Other Side: A Psychic's Tour of the Afterlife*. New York: New American Library, 2000.

Chopra, Deepak. *Life After Death: The Burden of Proof*. New York: Random House Inc., 2006.

Virtue, Doreen. *How to Hear Your Angels*. New York: Hay House, 2007.

Edward, John. *Crossing Over: The Stories Behind the Stories*. San Diego: Jodere Group Inc., 2001.

***

Charities List

American Cancer Society (www.cancer.org) is the place to go for cancer volunteerism information. Look for local chapters in your phonebook or online at this site.

The Boy Scouts of America and the Girl Scouts are great groups to get involved with if you looking for a quick way to help someone else. You can find either of them easily on the Internet (www.scouting.org or www.girlsouts.org) or by calling your nearby elementary school to find out if they have a troop affiliated with them.

If your good turn is to help someone who may be battling a terminal illness, visit www.caringbridge.org and www.carepages.com for ideas. Here they host free, personalized Web page space where you can create your own Web pages during a family member's critical illness, treatment or recovery to keep the burden off those affected who may not be able to update everyone when asked.

Goodwill Industries (www.Goodwill.org): Goodwill Industries International focuses on education, training and career services for disadvantaged people. They do this through offering donated pre-owned clothing and assorted household items to anyone recycling one's unused items for another's need. You can find Goodwill in your phonebook to donate your unwanted items as well as make a donation online.

The Humane Society (www.hsus.org) seeks to forge a lasting and comprehensive change in human consciousness of and behavior toward all animals in order to prevent animal cruelty, exploitation and neglect. They also serve to protect wild habitats and the entire community of life. The easiest place to start your search for your local animal shelter is online at www.Pets911.com.

iGive (www.igive.com) is a one-stop place to go for discovering all sorts of charities. Here you can find a charity of your choice and give financial support to them and receive savings by shopping at supporting businesses.

MADD (www.madd.org), or Mothers Against Drunk Driving, works hard on all aspects of eliminating drunk driving from our roads through activism, victim services and education.

Salvation Army (www.salvationarmyusa.org) is a charity army that is Christian-based and seeks to meet human needs without discrimination. Their services are wide-ranging, from national disaster relief serving thousands to individual support for job and housing services.

The United Way (www.unitedway.org): If you are interested in helping more than one charity at a time, this is the place. By volunteering at the United Way, your efforts spread to all of the charities they support.

YMCA/ YWCA (www.ymca.net or www.ywca.org): The YMCA has programs that build healthy spirit, mind and body for all. The YWCA is dedicated to eliminating racism, empowering women and promoting peace, justice, freedom and dignity for all. Regardless of your religious beliefs, either organization will help your community even more if you volunteer or donate to their cause.

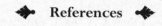

References

Chapter 5

Garcia, Elena. "Women More Likely Than Men to Pray, Believe in God". *Christian Post Reporter*, Tue, March 03 2009.

2008 U.S. Religious Landscape Survey, the Pew Forum, 2002 commentary for Gallup Poll.

Wijesinha, Sanfiva. "Can Faith Heal? Prayer and Meditation Certainly Influence Our Response to Illness." *Men's Health*, March 14, 2009.

Chapter 11

Widower Responses to the Death of a Wife: Findings (Authors and Disclosures), Topics in Advanced Practice Nursing eJournal, 2007; 7(2) copyright 2007 Medscape http://www.medscape.com/viewarticle/560196-4.

Chapter 24

Pennebaker, James W. *Writing to Heal: A Guided Journal for Recovering from Trauma and Emotional Upheaval*. Oakland, CA: New Harbinger Publications, Inc., 2004.

Chapter 25
Hales, Dianne. "Big Boys Don't Cry—and Other Myths About Men and
    Their Emotions. The truth about men, their emotions, and ways men
    can become more emotionally expressive." *Reader's Digest*, March 15,
    2009.

Chapter 28
Carney, Karen. "How Men Grieve." PsychCentral.com, April 12, 2000.

Chapter 29
Hayslip, Jr., Bert and Cynthia Peveto. *Cultural Changes in Attitudes Toward
    Death, Dying and Bereavement.* New York: Springer Publishing Company,
    2004.

Chapter 31
Harper, Jeanne M. "Men and Grief: Alpha Omega Venture."
    http://griefnet.org/library/griefgender.html.

Chapter 39
Gambill, Andrea. "Then and Now." http://thegriefblog.com/ (retrieved
    February 14, 2007).

Chapter 40
Parkside Memorial Funeral Home
    (http://www.parksidefuneralhome.com/_mgxroot/page_10729.html
    2007).
My Deepest Sympathy (http://mydeepestsympathy.com/comfort.aspx
    2008).

Chapter 41
Jrank.org. "Remarriage—Factors Affecting Likelihood Of Remarriage
    After Divorce Or Death of Spouse, Marital Relationships, Remarriage
    In Later Life." http://family.jrank.org/pages/1386/Remarriage.html.